The Admissions Counselor Malaise

Teege Mettille

Teege Enrollment Services, LLC
P.O. Box 568
Greendale, WI 53129
teegeenrollment.org

Published by Leading Colleges <05/15/2024>

9798323386659

DEDICATION

To every* admissions professional I've been fortunate enough to work with. Which, to the best of my recollection is Adrian, Alex, Alex, Alia, Alicia, Amanda, Amy, Andrea, Anissa, Anna, Anna, Annie, Annie, Ashley, Becky, Becky, Ben, Beth, Biagio, Billy, Brittany, Buffy, Carin, Carol, Chase, Chas, Cheryl, Cheryl Ann, Chuck, Cindy, Dave, Dawn, Dustin, Emily, Erika, Holly, Honey, Jacqueline, Jed, Jen, Jeron, Jillian, Jim, Kailagh, Kate, Katelyn, Kathy, Kelly, Ken, Kevin, Kris, Krista, Lee, Lee, Lezlie, Linda, Lori, Loutfi, Lynette, Lynn, Lynn, Lynn, Makaela, Marina, Matt, Miguel, Nathan, Nick, Nicole, Orlando, Oskar, Paris, Patty, Rick, Sadie, Sarah, Savannah, Sean, Seth, Shannon, Stacey, Steve, Susan, Tara, Teresa, Tori, Travis, and Whitney.

Of course, it would not be appropriate to write who my favorite was, but I am pretty sure that you know who you are.

* Also, please accept my deepest apologies to anyone I left off this list.

TEEGE METTILLE

THE MUCK

For months, before publishing this book, the main themes have been presented at various points. A webinar for members of the Chesapeake and Potomac Association of Collegiate Registrars and Admissions Officers (February, 2024). A session at the Southern Association for College Admission Counseling conference (March, 2024). As a keynote speech to end the Illinois Association for College Admission Counseling conference (April, 2024).

After each presentation, I took feedback to improve the message and delivery. While this feedback has me convinced that the general themes of this book are on to something, I was regularly receiving something akin to, "that was tough to sit through" or "it was a bummer."

To be clear, as best as I can tell, the feedback was not related to my presentation style or the validity of the points you are about to read. Instead, the process of walking through and recognizing the deep-seeded causes of *The Admissions Counselor Malaise* is difficult to go through.

Which is where this book is about to take you.

My hope is that by taking you on this journey of where our profession has gone astray from the core values of the professionals involved, you'll be able to better assess what's actually impacting you and your colleagues. Unfortunately, I do not know a way to bring you to that clarity without first taking you through the muck of these transitions.

Please know, there *are* solutions at the end. In fact, feel free to skip ahead at any point you need some optimism and levity.

And there is optimism at the end. I really do believe that in spite of the challenges we face, there's hope for us. We can hold on to the core values we each bring to this work *and* meet institutional revenue needs at the same time. While this book appears to pitch those two competing demands as oppositional to each other, that comes as an observation, not a statement of fact.

We can align our work and our values again.

We'll all be happier when we do.

With Appreciation

About The Author

THE PURPOSE OF THIS BOOK

Since the rise of the pandemic, something has been bothering me about the profession of college admissions.

By that, I don't mean to take issue with many of the decisions we had to make in a haphazard, quick way that lacked the research and intentionality we are used to. For example, the disorganized and confusing adoption of test optional policies, the easy relinquishing of NACAC's Statement of Principles and Good Practice, or even the impossible pressure from college Presidents, Chancellors, and boards to ensure that somehow, the pandemic not impact enrollment revenue.

While all of those are issues that we could discuss - there's something more fundamental to our work that is lacking.

Admissions counselors do not like their jobs anymore.

A bold statement, to be sure, but one that I think is imminently defensible. In fact, I will spend this entire text defending that core assumption. So, let's get a few things out of the way about this, as it is the fundamental belief upon which everything else I argue for is built.

> No, the morale issues are not exclusive to admissions counselors - it has invaded all levels of admissions leadership.

No, the morale issues are not unique to the college-side of the desk either - school counselors, independent educational consultants, and community-based organization professionals are also feeling the sting of our current climate.

No, this is not all inclusive. A profession with tens of thousands of members will necessarily have hundreds if not thousands of exceptions.

With those caveats stated, let me say again, something has changed in our profession, and admissions counselors are just not happy.

The evidence is all around us - although our collective focus has been fading. Staff morale crises, employee turnover, counselors willing to quit right in the middle of yield season. Have we ever seen this so broadly before?

We have not - because unlike in the past, admissions counselors do not like their jobs anymore.

You can see the truth of this statement in watching counselors struggle with the return of fall travel.

You can see the truth of this statement as they question the morality of asking students to take on *any* amount of student loan debt.

You can see the truth of this statement as they tell you from day one that they are underpaid for the emotional labor they are bringing to their work.

In the last two years, I've had many windows into the view admissions leaders have on this issue. As co-host of The Admissions Directors Lunchcast, the off-mic conversations are often more enlightening about what's happening than the recorded ones. As the pandemic raged on, I returned for nine months as the past president of the Wisconsin Association for

College Admission Counseling, maintaining contact with leaders in the state and members of NACAC's President's Council. On two college campuses, in Wisconsin and Indiana, I saw what was happening through my own lens. Since leaving campus, I've had a consulting relationship with about two dozen admissions leaders through Leading Colleges and my work with enroll ml.

Through these various roles, I've listened to many Vice Presidents of Enrollment, Deans and Directors of Admissions, and even senior-level counselors complain about the problem. Stories abound of young admissions counselors being ungrateful for their job, unappreciative of their leadership, and a seeming disregard for the needs of the institution. These conversations are not hard to find - in fact, in the last few years, they're hard to avoid.

Admissions leaders, and college leaders generally, have come to blame admissions counselors. Today's admissions counselors have access to more tools, more resources, and more conveniences to do their work than ever before. Admissions leaders reflect to their time as new professionals the same way my parents did when talking about how far they walked to school when they were kids - with a firm "kids today" attitude.

We are wrong to blame admissions counselors.

The truth is we are collectively failing our admissions counselors.

More concerningly, we don't currently have a clear understanding of *why* we are failing them. We recognize the problem, but it has no name, no clear cause, no evident solutions. It's not to suggest we haven't been trying - isolated efforts of changed work/life balance, flexible work from home policies, even reduced travel and outreach expectations have been implemented, to no avail. The solutions haven't worked. And they won't work, until we better understand what the problem really is. Unfortunately, we can't ask counselors to tell us directly, because as has always been the case with a problem with no name, they don't yet have the words for it.

In this book, I'll endeavor to work through these challenging issues in a new way - zeroing in on root causes. Evaluating new ways of analyzing the problem. Hopefully, a few solutions will emerge by standing on the shoulders of a giant in the feminist movement. Betty Friedan, author of *The Feminine Mystique*, was one of the instigators of the second-wave of the feminist movement in the United States. Her work, her insights, and her perspective, while flawed, helped our society understand a social issue never clearly defined before.

Believe it or not, the admissions staff morale crisis that you read about, talk about, and have probably experienced for yourself, can be better analyzed by finding parallel experiences with the plight of suburban housewives in 1950s America.

When Betty Friedan published *The Feminine Mystique* in 1963, she identified "a problem that has no name." My goal for this work is to play my part in doing that for our profession - to name it, allowing us all to claim it, so we can collectively reframe it.

Roseanne.
Tupperware.
Change.

In the 1980s, a sitcom based on the life of Roseanne Barr burst into mainstream society, becoming one of the most popular television shows of the time. As the show's popularity hit its zenith, Roseanne herself became one of the most polarizing figures in America. That of course pales in comparison to the public statements she made about Valerie Jarrett in 2018. Her comments were widely panned as problematic and racist (including by me). It is unfortunate that she chose to use her public stage as she did, because her work in the 1980s was quite influential in the public dialogue of the role of women at the time, especially as it related to women in leadership and working-class women.

Much of it still stands the test of time. Specifically, as it relates to this book, there is one scene that is particularly impactful. I'll do my best to describe it - although it will come to life more if you have at least a passing awareness of Roseanne, and her character's sister, Jackie, from the television show. The scene, which lasts less than 2 minutes, happens like this.

The image is black and white, indicating that this is a flashback to the 1950s, approximately 30 years prior. Roseanne is wearing a full dress, complete with an apron that can best be described as formal, frilly, and freshly cleaned. Jackie is wearing a blouse adorned with butterflies, the cursive letter "J", and her hair in tight curlers. The scene begins around the table in Roseanne's kitchen.

Roseanne: *(Her voice is stressed, her face is pained, she is ringing her hands)* ...I balance the checkbook, I do the shopping, and I take care of the kids and the car, and darn it, I'm just not...

Jackie: *(Leaning in, her voice is elevated, quickened)* Say it, Rosie! Say it!

Roseanne: I'm just not happy! *(She looks frightened, both hands cover her mouth, as if attempting to put the words back)*

Jackie: *(Stands up a bit straighter, her face shows resolve)* That's all I needed to hear.

The music changes to a drumbeat while Jackie walks through the kitchen, closing blinds and doors, so she can speak privately with Roseanne.

Roseanne: Jackie, what are you doing?

Jackie: You are not alone, there are other women who feel the way that you do. They talk about changing things.

Roseanne: *(With concern)* Changing things?!?

Jackie: Who don't want to take it anymore!

Roseanne: No, stop!

Jackie: Who don't want to do what their husbands say just because they say so!

Roseanne: *(Her hands are waving in the air as if she is attempting to keep the ideas at bay)* No more! No more! You're giving me a pounding headache!

Jackie: *(Coming closer to Roseanne, shaking her by the shoulders)* I'm not giving you a headache, the truth is giving you a headache!

Roseanne: Jackie, I can't believe this is coming from you. You're so wacky!

Jackie: *(Wild eyed, looking to the side)* That's my cover! A bunch of us are having meetings, once a week. We call them 'Tupperware Parties.'

(Roseanne's face is frozen, allowing this to wash over her)

Jackie: *(Finger waving, standing even firmer, to underscore her belief in change.)* There's only a few of us now, but we're growing. We're planning a revolution!

Roseanne: *(Looking shocked, mouth agape)* Under the guise of keeping your leftovers fresh? *(Her shocked expression turns to impressed appreciation; her breathing begins to slow)* That's brilliant!

Jackie: *(Smiling broadly, then she suddenly becomes much more serious, recognizing the precariousness of her next question.)* Are you with us?

Roseanne: *(Holding her hands to her chest)* Are you telling me that if I join, I…I won't have this feeling of hopelessness anymore, I…I can have some control in my own life, and my own destiny?

Jackie: *(Lightly bouncing in her excitement)* YES! That's the spirit, sister! *(She holds a clenched fist in the air)*

Roseanne: *(Looking concerned, steps back)* Well, you're not going to hit me, are you?

Jackie: No, no! This is what we all do!

TEEGE METTILLE

A TENUOUS CONNECTION

Of course, making a connection between two disparate groups, separated culturally, emotionally, and chronologically (by 70 years!) can be a strained perspective. But it is a perspective that is not just well founded, it can be particularly powerful in illuminating the solutions we need. To understand the relationship between these two seemingly disconnected groups (1950s suburban housewives and young admissions counselors in 2024) we need to understand what Betty Friedan was telling us in *The Feminine Mystique*.

Throughout this book, we will travel back and forth between these two worlds - visiting the world of our grandmothers (or great-grandmothers!) before coming back to our modern world. With each trip through time, we will work to apply the lessons from the past to our current challenges, allowing us to review and evaluate people, problems, organizations, and challenges in a new and more effective way.

Understanding The Feminine Mystique

To fully embrace Friedan's lessons, it will be helpful to start with a visualization. Take the phrase "1950s suburban housewife" - and consider who comes to mind. Really spend a few minutes on this.

The typical suburban housewife of the time - who is she?

What motivates her?

What is her family structure?

What role does she play in society?

How does that compare to her mother and grandmothers?

How did she find herself in the situation she is in?

What makes her happy?

Is she happy?

Throughout this text, it will be helpful to call back on the answers you generated to these questions. It will allow you to humanize the societal challenge that is discussed by Friedan in a way that can sometimes seem more academic and theoretical. There were real women with hopes, dreams, challenges, and ambitions behind every concept she raises. We will get through many of her main ideas, but the 30,000-foot view will allow us to begin.

After the passage of the 19th amendment, where women successfully claimed the right to vote, their role in society was beginning to settle into new norms. Women had not just earned the vote, they earned seats at college campuses, in the world of work, in society generally. In fact, the image many of us conjure up when imagining the 1950s suburban housewife, as portrayed in the scene from *Roseanne*, can best be considered a reversion. Friedan regularly says that the 1950s suburban housewife made the decision to "return to the home."

It happened at the conclusion of a global war, which created significant disruption in societal and gender roles. With men being sent overseas, the women left behind found new roles and a greater sense of purpose than they had previously experienced. Of course this is typified with Rosie the Riveter, but it ran much deeper. Even something as simple as growing carrots and a few heads of lettuce was rebranded. This "Victory Garden" encouraged the women tending their backyard produce to see that work as contributing to the war effort. During the war, gardening wasn't just a hobby, it was part of that woman's contribution to saving the world from the rule of a Fascist dictator.

World War II ended, the men returned to their homes, and the Victory Garden lost its sense of purpose. It once again became true that gardening was a relatively meaningless activity in the grand scheme of things. Society didn't return to "normal" - but it did attempt to create a new normal. Suburbs exploded all over the country, the GI Bill created educational opportunities and the ranks of "suburban housewives" swelled in numbers."

The Feminine Mystique was not about capturing the plight of women making the slow but continuous march closer towards equality and independence. Instead, it was a comprehensive, academic, and indicting evaluation of why an entire sub-population made the decision to give up societal advancements won by the women who came before them.

It is also worth noting (and perhaps considering if it's more than coincidental) that there was no significant feminist movement for thirty years before the emergence of the 1950s suburban housewife.

As is humorously dramatized in the scene from Roseanne 30 years ago, women of the time felt a sense of unhappiness, a profound lack of fulfillment in their lives. However, because so many people in the suburbs performed happiness for their neighbors, they felt alone. There was a crushing feeling of isolation for any individual woman feeling this way. There were few avenues to find understanding. Turning to older women in their lives would have been no help, as the experience of the 1950s suburban housewives had to appear dreamlike to women just a generation before *and* a choice each woman made.

So, for fifteen years after World War II ended, suburban housewives would have felt alone because there was no reason to come to any other conclusion. They were made to feel like there was something wrong with them. If they dared raise their feelings to trusted friends or relatives, they could expect to be made to feel worse, because their sense of happiness and fulfillment was supposed to be about being a good wife and mother. If you weren't happy or satisfied in those roles, were you failing?

1950s suburban housewives were being told that their personal happiness, sense of purpose and fulfillment, was dependent on the well-being of other people.

It's not about you, it's about your kids.

It's not about you, it's about your husband.

It's not about your goals, it's about your husband's career.

If things are going well for them, they're going well for you.

If they're happy, that should be enough for you.

It wasn't.

Criticism of The Feminine Mystique

Let's address this at the outset. *The Feminine Mystique* does not capture the experience of women in America in the 1950s. It doesn't even capture the experience of most of them. Instead, this book is diving deep on one sub-population of that group - 1950s suburban housewives. Implicit in that categorization are the following characteristics that define these women:

- White
- Middle-Class
- Mothers
- Heterosexual
- Married

In addition to those five qualities, Friedan's work keeps most of its focus on women of the time who chose to become 1950s suburban housewives even with the benefit of a college education. So, to round out the list of limiting characteristics of who she is analyzing, add: college-educated.

The criticism of Friedan's work is both correct and appropriate, but Friedan never presented her analysis as anything other than analyzing this small group of people. While I will refer to 1950s suburban housewives throughout this book, know that the six characteristics listed above are infused into the category.

What's Happening to Admissions Counselors?

If not immediately apparent, it doesn't take long to connect the experience of 1950s suburban housewives with modern day admissions counselors. From my experience at four different institutions and consulting with dozens more, I offer the following observations:

While our profession has always been evolving, the rate of change accelerated about 20 years ago. Just as *College Unranked*, edited by Lloyd Thacker was published to contribute to the debate about the commercialization of higher education, the modern CRM was coming online. About 15 years ago, the most consequential of them, Slate, started to take its place as a leader in the market. Suddenly, as college was increasingly becoming a commodity, financial aid became a lure for the wealthy more than a helping hand for those in need, and colleges began amassing an enormous data warehouse on each individual student.

Each year, our profession took one or two steps away from where we had been in the past. The 2008 version of NACAC's SPGP, which previously served as our guiding ethical document, became just a little quainter and more difficult to connect with each year. Since each new cycle was just one or two steps along the path of change, we never really noticed how significant the building change was becoming.

Each year, we became a little more focused on a discounting model that rewards wealth over need.

Each year, we became a little more focused on converting more applicants into paying students.

Each year, we became a little more focused on recruiting students with a more substantial ability to pay.

Each year, we became a little more focused on growing the applicant pool without growing the admissions counseling team at the same rate.

Each year, we became a little more focused on queries and using our data warehouse to target students out of applicant pools that grew increasingly too large to manage.

Each year, we became a little *less* focused on each student as an individual with goals, hopes, dreams, and ambitions unique to them.

Yet we never changed who we were hiring.

We continued to hire people to be admissions counselors who are effervescent, engaging, energetic, and eager to connect with students.

We continued to hire people to be admissions counselors who are excited to make a difference in the lives of young people, to provide access to higher education.

We continued to hire people who believed they were joining one of the helping professions.

Then, as happened to the 1950s suburban housewives, there was an incendiary incident that changed everything. As World War II shook up society and changed how women viewed their role in society, COVID-19 shook up college admissions offices and changed how admissions counselors view their work.

The new sense of purpose, autonomy, freedom, the sense of control over our own work / life balance that existed during the social distancing era fundamentally altered everyone's outlook on work. For admissions counselors, it removed them from committee meetings, separated them from water cooler conversations about discount rates or TikTok trends, and encouraged them to find new ways to connect with students.

Those new ways of connecting with students operated like the Victory Gardens of 80 years ago. During the social distancing era, zoom meetings reminded counselors of the greater purpose of their work - it is not to generate a marginal increase on the net tuition revenue rate for their institution. Their greater purpose was to make a difference. That's what attracted them to this work to begin with, and until they were sent home to sit alone in a zoom, they didn't see clearly how far we had drifted from that.

The ability to make a difference in the lives of students is why they're with us. For those few months of working from home, they could dial in to work that mattered, and dial out of work that didn't.

So, when the social distancing era of the pandemic was drawn down and college leadership wanted things to go back to the way they were, counselors revolted. Or, got as close to revolting as you can in an area where unionization and collective bargaining is rare and staying that way. Without a formal structure for revolting - and lacking the organizational structure of "Tupperware Parties" - their revolt looks like a massive staff morale and employee turnover crisis hurting college admissions offices everywhere.

Those of us who have been through enough admissions cycles to remember how the 2008 housing market crash impacted admissions are right to be confused. From our perspective, counselors today seem to have it so much easier than we ever did. They have more tools, better research, slicker materials, better buildings. They don't even remember a travel season before GPS and it wouldn't need to occur to them to look for the football stadium lights. In our quiet conversations away from new admissions counselors, we often find ourselves asking why they are so unhappy with their jobs.

Today, if you ask counselors what would make their jobs better, they will give you an answer. They may say that they want flexibility to work from home. They may say that they want a better work / life balance. They may say that they need more pay for the work that they do. Yet, as was discussed at NACAC's 2023 National Conference, in a case study where those changes were made, *admissions counselors remained unhappy with their work.*

They are not unhappy because of requirements to return to the office, although those are quaint and should be updated.

They are not unhappy because of their work / life balance, although it is out of whack and needs to be corrected.

They are not unhappy because they are underpaid, although they are, and we need to fix that problem as soon as possible.

They are unhappy because COVID-19 showed us the power of personal, human connection, and the way it can help admissions counselors and students alike - and they want that connection back. Today's admissions counselors want to make a difference for the lives of students far more than they want to make a difference in the budgeting process for your campus' political science department.

They want to feel like their work has purpose and meaning.

For 1950s suburban housewives, the deep sense of unhappiness, the lack of fulfillment, this "problem that has no name" came to be understood colloquially as *The Feminine Mystique.*

In 2024, admissions counselors have a deep sense of unhappiness, a lack of fulfillment in their work, and a feeling that something is awry and needs to be fixed.

That is *The Admissions Counselor Malaise.*

TEEGE METTILLE

SACRIFICE

If there is a simple, core connection between *The Admissions Counselor Malaise* and *The Feminine Mystique*, it is this: both groups being written about were asked to abandon a drive towards personal fulfillment in favor of those whose care they were responsible for. The 1950s suburban housewives were asked to sacrifice for their children, their husband, and the institution of marriage. Post-COVID admissions counselors are asked to sacrifice for their students, their President, and the institution for which they work.

In both cases, the request to give up on personal fulfillment didn't come lightly, or without reason. In fact, the institutions they were involved with had been built in such a way that this abandonment was necessary to achieve specific goals. At the same time, in both cases, the drive for personal fulfillment cannot be fully abandoned. If it could, there would not have been a profound sense of unhappiness in 1950s suburban housewives or post-COVID admissions counselors. No matter how necessary the increase in net tuition revenue or freshly ironed bed sheets (yes, they did that) - the drive towards personal fulfillment is too strong to be fully extinguished.

So, what happens when there is a disconnect between the needs of the institution (whether that be the institution of marriage or an institution of higher learning) and the pathways for individuals within to find fulfillment, satisfaction, and a strong sense of purpose?

Of course, a sacrifice will be made, and it will be made by the individual. There is no institution that will allow itself to be on the wrong end of that scale. Instead, the institution will demand of its members a personal sacrifice for the good of the whole. This requirement will be couched in terms of altruism, an appeal to the greater good, but make no mistake - the institution will never take a loss for the benefit of the individuals within it. The institution would sooner replace the individuals.

This is the power of institutional will. While these institutions are set up by individuals, there becomes a collective will that overpowers individual concerns. Throughout history, at times in our darkest hours, this truism has shown itself repeatedly. For 1950s suburban housewives, the institutions demanded them to play a role, and so they did. For post-COVID admissions counselors, the institutions demand them to approach their work in a specific way, and so they do. Or they leave, replaced by someone else who will, at least for a short period of time.

This is one of the problems with no name that we are wrestling with in college admissions. For reasons we all know and understand, there is an unquenched thirst on college campuses for "more." More revenue, more students, more market share. The institutions are set up to chase after that thirst, no matter what the cost to the individuals involved. After all, the individuals can (and will) be replaced, but the institution must continue.

To be clear, the language in the previous paragraph was intentionally precise. The word "unquenched" is to stress a reality we all face - no matter how well an admissions office does, next year, the goal is to find more. I've managed admissions teams when we have far exceeded the goal of students and revenue, and I've managed teams when we have landed far short of the goal of students and revenue. In both cases, the charge next year was the same: *more.* The thirst for revenue isn't unquenchable - we can meet the stated goals. Yet every successful admissions leader will tell you that somehow, invariably, next year, we need more.

The lack of nuance in the phrase "no matter the cost to individuals involved" was intentionally void of nuance. Institutions will pursue their unending revenue needs with no shame in asking for sacrifice from faculty and staff, including admissions counselors. However, these aren't the only individuals involved - students and families, school counselors, independent educational consultants, community-based organization professionals - that sentence is meant to include every single person involved in the work of colleges. The drive for *more* will not stop, no matter how much we need to ask everyone to sacrifice for the greater good.

This admittedly places the role of college leadership in stark terms.

What other conclusions can we come to?

At the annual NACAC conference in 2023, there was a seemingly unending parade of sessions on issues related to what I now refer to as *The Admissions Counselor Malaise.* Staff morale, turnover, employee engagement - all different sides of the same issue. After attending several of the sessions (and presenting one myself!) - I left with a core question. It has been gnawing at me since before my flight left Baltimore to return to the relative calm of the Midwest at the start of a surprisingly mild fall.

I came to understand that the work / life balance expectations of colleges and universities is one of the core challenges admissions counselors are facing. Yet the challenge our profession is trying to solve is *not* the unsustainability of those expectations - but the fact that new admissions counselors are roundly rejecting these expectations in ways they never have before. New admissions counselors are leaving for better paying jobs, with more reasonable expectations if needed. Or, perhaps worse, they remain in their jobs and choose to meet their internal expectations instead. I suspect this is happening because admissions leaders are, by and large, not able to change the work / life balance expectations demanded of our current workforce. Which begs the question:

Have colleges and universities built a recruitment model that *requires* an unhealthy work / life balance from admissions counselors?

It's Really All About the Children

A review of Betty Friedan's work underscores one of the most insidious elements of the pressures placed on 1950s suburban housewives. Throughout *The Feminine Mystique*, Friedan catalogs countless examples of popular culture and mass media reinforcing the refrain that later became the mantra of "I believe the children are the future." It made clear that raising children successfully, in and of itself, should provide a sense of purpose and meaning in a woman's life.

The 1950s suburban housewives found numbing monotony in their lives - going through each day in a harried, always busy, never productive, way, ending each day exhausted, staring at the ceiling, asking themselves, "is this it?"

This is despite having access to tools and technology that were unavailable to the women who came before them.

This is despite having access to (and in many cases, achieving) a college education that would grant them entry to fulfilling work.

This is despite genuinely believing that their children were in fact the most important job they will have.

Despite all of that, even with mass media reinforcement, the question remained.

Is this it?

Of course, the institutions of family and marriage at the time could not have women contemplating that question. The disruption, if it took root, would be too much for the institution to bear. Instead, the individuals operating within the institutions need to carry the weight of problems that were not of their making. Making this possible was a stream of articles, cute stories, radio, and television specials all depicting what Friedan referred to as the Housewife

Heroine - a "woman who was so naturally happy to devote her life to her husband and children, she didn't need anything else."

This imagery, this perception, was normalized. People came to believe that this wasn't just the ideal, it was the reality for women serving as 1950s suburban housewives. Any time a woman living through that began to question the value or the purpose of her role in society - the answer came through loud and clear: it's really all about the children. This was a near-universal answer to anyone experiencing *The Feminine Mystique* - be happy for the home you are providing your children. Be happy for the life you are providing your children. Be happy for the future you are creating for your children.

It all came back to the children.

This created situations where women who felt unfulfilled were made to feel like "bad mothers" - a label worse than the scarlet letter. Of course, being labeled a bad mother at any point in our history is not good - it's certainly not something we would be comfortable being reported about us today. That said, it would be a mistake and a misread to presume that this phrase is just as powerful for us today as it was for 1950s suburban housewives. The aversion to that slur must have been stronger and more constant than we could imagine today. Perhaps, the desire to avoid that label was overwhelming enough to get them to accept the personal sacrifice that the institutions they were playing a part in demanded of them.

It really is easy to think back and imagine that the world was so radically different, and that suddenly, 1950s suburban housewives just dreamed of a more interesting, purposeful life. However, as discussed in the introduction, that would miss the experience of women from the generation preceding World War II.

After the suffrage movement declared victory (although a more appropriate analysis would be that it was victorious in securing the right to vote for white women) - women in the 1920s and 1930s had been perceived as liberated. In many ways, white women were, at least freed from the constraints from the generations before them. Friedan herself suggests that obstacles to equality in society had been overcome - and yet, after the war, many women chose to go back to the home.

In the opening paragraphs of *The Feminine Mystique,* Friedan notes that while the number of women achieving increasing levels of education rose, many of those women were giving up their individual professional pursuits in favor of finding a husband and starting a family. In short, they were giving up some of the freedoms won for them by their mothers and grandmothers. In fact, one could argue that people reading this book in 2024 would more quickly recognize the experience of women in the 1930s than the 1950s. It is not correct to think that *The Feminine Mystique* represents an uprising from women who had finally hit their limit with the outdated roles they were placed in.

It's almost as if these women answered a call from some unknown force to Make Homemaking Great Again.

So, when we imagine the impact of a "bad mother" label or the desire to fulfill a role in the institutions of marriage and family, we must remember that it was not preordained that they be in this role. As Friedan chronicled, for this group of women, this was a choice. Not only did they have a role to play, but if they failed, it would also mean they made a mistake in determining the trajectory of their life.

Whatever the reason, the dissatisfaction, the lack of fulfillment, the nagging, constant question of, "is this all" - it all existed for a reason. Institutional stability demanded it. Institutions would crumble without it. And most importantly, the children would suffer.

Because after all, it really is about the children.

Right?

It's Really All About the Students

This next section could almost write itself. The similarities, the parallel tracks, everything is the same story, just seventy years later. Admissions counselors today are people, individuals, deserving of professional fulfillment, personal satisfaction, and yes, happiness in their job, *regardless of how that impacts students.*

In 2024, the narrative that everything we do is really about the students is so pervasive, it seems almost heretical to even hint at a counter narrative, much less to outright make the case for it. For too long, our profession has relied on admissions counselors sacrificing themselves for the greater good of the institution. It's gone on so long that the entire infrastructure behind our institutions of higher learning is built on top of a foundation of an unhealthy work / life balance in the admissions office. So, the institution demands this personal sacrifice of its admissions counselors, but makes the request (demand?) under the guise of "for the students" where "for the institution" wouldn't work. After all, how many admissions professionals are drawn to this work for reasons other than serving students well?

This is a combination of groupthink and gaslighting - a toxic slurry of damaged thought processes that our profession is trying to muddle through. Of course, if you ask an admissions professional why they are in their role, they will cite students, almost immediately. This is nearly without exception, and easy to see. Try it right now - email five admissions professionals and ask them what brought them to their work. It is unlikely that five out of five won't respond with some version of "to help students." Four out of five will be rare. Three out of five is just plain unlikely.

But could it be possible that there are other reasons we are drawn to this work besides serving students well? Those reasons would be tucked below the surface, because we all begin and many of us end with "to help students." Perhaps, there are other reasons, but the culture in our profession is so strong, so pervasive, so absolutely insistent that the work we do is "to help students" first and foremost, that we all learn to repeat it. Almost like a pledge, recited without meaning or intention, because it is the accepted professional script. In following the script, we protect our personal positions, but we also play our part in reinforcing the institutional imperative to make sacrifices for the benefit of the students we serve.

1950s suburban housewives performed happiness for each other, making anyone who didn't genuinely feel the correct way view themselves as an outcast, defective, a failure. Are today's admissions counselors conflicting a similar mindset on each other?

Perhaps our profession just does a great job weeding out people early and often who are not student centric. Getting rid of people who are not motivated first and foremost (and secondarily and supplementarily) by making sure every decision benefits our students. After all, as the signs you sometimes see on campuses say, students are not an interruption to our work, they are the reason for it!

Or, perhaps, from before we even come for the interview, we know that performing not just a students-first attitude, but a *students-only attitude* is a requirement for getting the job, keeping the job, and getting promoted in the job. Maybe, just maybe, admissions professionals have personal goals, ambitions, and purposes that are disconnected from how those goals impact students.

Is that possible?

Is that likely?

More pressing: is that allowable?

In today's environment, it is not. Much like 1950s suburban housewives played their part for each other, thereby contributing to the problem for others as others returned the favor, admissions counselors are doing the same thing. By performing "it's really all about the students" for each other, we create a social environment where any other motivation is suspect and cast as shady, just by virtue of being outside the prevailing narrative that we all pledge on repeat.

We perform it so much, so consistently, so regularly, so routinely, that no one questions it.

But if this is as true as we all have believed (me included) - why is it that there is a pervasive sense of unhappiness among our workforce?

If this is true, why is it that there is a turnover crisis in college admissions offices that seemed to take over the session selection process for NACAC 2022 and 2023?

If this is true, why is it that The Chronicle of Higher Education could write a new story every day about this problem, and not run out of anecdotes, examples, case studies, and theories?

Let me be clear - this argument is not to suggest that we abandon students, or that we shouldn't be considering them when we are making decisions on policies, procedures, program offerings, and pricing. Instead, the argument is that we will better serve our admissions counseling professionals if we stop pretending that it is the *only* consideration.

It's long since been true that students are not the first, second, and third consideration colleges have as they continue to build on the legacy and history of their institutions. It may even be true that students are no longer the first consideration our profession has when making decisions. For many of us, the first consideration is not the impact on students, but the impact on revenue - an infectious mindset that has spread from the cabinet to the admissions office. With increasing frequency, the financial needs of the institution are at the fore of the conversation before the impact on student experience. That's why, on college campuses across the country, everything, even something as mundane as determining which parking lot to resurface next summer, is pitched to the Vice President of Enrollment as a moment to provide guidance as to which parking lot would be "better for enrollment."

Because campus leadership has abandoned a "students-only" mindset, and in many cases, even a "students-first" mindset. It's become clear that major decisions are being made not from a student-centric perspective, but from a revenue-centric perspective. When everyone was performing "it's all about the students" - admissions counselors could find their place in that mindset. When their campus leadership has demonstrated repeatedly that they're taking a different approach, it calls into question the entire script.

The financial needs of the institution don't just rival the needs of the student - they trump them. We know that this is nearly universally true at this point - and we come up with all sorts of rationalizations to make it okay.

"No margin, no mission."

"We can't serve students if we can't pay our bills."

"A higher ranking ultimately benefits our students."

"We don't have the endowment to do it differently."

It's all rationalization, designed to make us feel better about moving in a direction that we know in our soul is not correct. When we made student needs secondary to institutional needs in nearly every decision, we created cognitive dissonance that we needed to wrestle with. That's understandable, but it's time to reassess our mindset.

These arguments are not meant to suggest that the needs of the student shouldn't be a central consideration in our mind - it should be. It's also appropriate that the needs of the institution should be a central consideration - and we don't need to develop increasingly strained rationalizations to feel okay about it. But it is also appropriate, indeed it is necessary, to consider the needs of our staff as a central consideration as well.

It is not anti-institution or anti-student to suggest that the college should serve the needs of the faculty and staff that work there.

Our recruitment models are built upon the idea that there are eager, energetic, enthusiastic young admissions professionals who will embrace an unhealthy work / life balance for the benefit of students. That worked for a long time - but it no longer is, and here's why: our admissions counselors no longer believe that their colleges and universities are centering students first and foremost. Once that perception hit admissions counselors, the demand for personal sacrifice loses its moral certitude and persuasion.

Admissions counselors have seen that the institution is looking beyond the needs of students when making significant decisions. It is leading them to be disillusioned about the institution they are working to uplift and uphold.

If the institution is asking about the enrollment impact of whether to offer a fourth day of on-campus orientation *before* asking about the impact on the student experience - the counselors can and do intuit that the answer is not about the student.

If the institution is asking about the enrollment impact of adding or removing three tenure-track faculty positions compared to adjunct positions *before* asking about the impact on the student experience - the counselors can and do intuit that the answer is not about the student.

If the institution is asking about the enrollment impact of investing $1,000,000 in an expensive student search campaign *before* asking about the impact on the student experience - the counselors can and do intuit that the answer is not about the student.

If the college is asking about the enrollment impact of completing a tuition reset *before* asking about the impact on the student experience - the counselors can and do intuit that the answer is not about the student.

If the college is asking about the enrollment impact of switching to online learning during COVID *before* asking about the impact on the student experience - the counselors can and do intuit that the answer is not about the student.

None of this is to say that the enrollment impact shouldn't be factored into these decisions. It should - it's critical. But we all know that for many of these questions, it's not just that institutional imperatives are considered before evaluating the impact to students. Leaders in our profession know in our gut that the answer to how these decisions will impact students is often irrelevant. If it leads to more revenue, the institution is going to do it.

"No margin, no mission."

"We can't serve students if we can't pay our bills."

"A higher ranking ultimately benefits our students."

"We don't have the endowment to do it differently."

So, when an institution asks its staff to dig deeper, give more, sacrifice another Saturday away from their lives, stay late for a calling campaign - for the benefit of the students - it rings hollow. If admissions counselors are performing a students-first mindset for each other the way 1950s suburban housewives performed happiness for each other, the perceived institutional abandonment of that mindset shatters the illusion.

Institutions who have stopped centering the student experience in their major decisions (or are perceived as such by counselors) do not have credibility when asking staff to keep doing so. They then fall on mission-driven gaslighting - a phrase that is conceptualized as the antithesis to "it's all about students." If institutional leadership seems to be here to run up revenues first, *using students to do so,* then why is it so inappropriate for admissions counselors to call BS? Why is it so inappropriate for admissions counselors to question the sacrifice / reward balance of their job? Why is it so inappropriate for admissions counselors to be unhappy?

Admissions counselors are people, too. They have inherent value, and are just as deserving of respect, personal fulfillment, and happiness as the students they were just a few years ago. It's not just appropriate for us to recognize that - it's imperative that we do. Once we do, giving them (and other campus staff) their rightful place at the center of our decision-making tables, alongside student needs and institutional imperatives, we will see different outcomes.

The alternative is to just keep repeating the same tired line that got us in this mess - because we kept repeating it long after we stopped living it.

It's all about the students.

Right?

INCENDIARY INCIDENTS

There are many vexing aspects of The Admissions Counselor Malaise for those who are tasked with curing it. Among the most difficult to understand: where did it come from and why is it so intractable? After attending several sessions, reading articles, scouring blog posts, and listening to podcasts on the topic, it seems that we are no closer to understanding the root cause of the issue. How did an entire profession, an entire group of young professionals, sour on their work so quickly, so deeply, so uniformly? More confusing: how is it that new admissions counselors who did not live through the changes of the last five years also come to share in the sentiment?

Of course, many people have pointed to COVID-19 as the cause. The challenge of converting back from work-from-home policies has frustrated people, who would prefer not to return to the office. This theory misses the mark - a fact that is self-evident when you realize that new admissions counselors, hired after the social distancing era, seem to be just as dissatisfied with our work than we remember being true before.

Recency bias or self-selection bias are sometimes considered as reasonable explanations as well. Perhaps it has always been this way, we are just feeling it more because it is current. These theories miss the mark, too. We do not need to conduct several years of research to know that *we never used to start counselors in November, January, and March!* At least, not as a standard course of action. While there are and were always exceptions, as a rule, you could plan to start the fall with a full team, having had more than enough applicants to choose from, and that your team would stay largely intact through May. When a counselor starts in August and quits in October, it's not recency bias that causes you to question what's changed - it's reality.

For many people looking for solutions to The Admissions Counselor Malaise, pointing to the pandemic makes intuitive sense. The problems came to the surface during social distancing, and just haven't retreated. But we are fundamentally misunderstanding the role of the pandemic in this problem. Misattribution error is in full force. The pandemic isn't the cause of the malaise, it is the incendiary incident that helped us see it.

It is the spark that allowed us to see what was burning below the surface. The pandemic didn't start this fire - it was always burning. The difference is that now, we see it.

World War II

So far, we have reviewed the history of women's rights leading into the 1950s with passing awareness. To fully understand the impact of an incendiary incident in identifying a problem that has no name, we need to dig deeper on the history of the rights of women, the women's rights movement, and how 1950s suburban housewives found themselves in the situation they were in.

Remember, *The Feminine Mystique* is credited as a launching point for the second wave of the feminist movement. This definitionally implies that there was a first, and that there was a gap between the two waves. While this is not meant to be a comprehensive view of the feminist movements in the United States, there are some key moments highlighted for the purpose of understanding the framing of World War II as an incendiary incident.

At Seneca Falls, New York, in 1840, the Women's Suffrage movement was launched. If you haven't done so already (or recently), review some of the historic accounts of that convention. The speeches, the speakers, the audience - in reading about them 175 years later, they seem so eclectic. So alive with possibility, progress, and potential. This moment put into motion the long, painstaking, halting progress that ultimately culminated with the passage of the 19th amendment, 72 years later. Literally generations of women were involved in the fight - in some cases, the leaders of the movement at its successful end were the children and grandchildren of the women who originally led the charge.

After that long fight, one can only imagine that the women who pushed through this change were tired. They had more than earned the right to step back - to move on and enjoy the victory. Of course, the right to vote was technically secured for all women, but many women were still denied the right to vote until the passage of the Voting Rights act another two generations later. Still, rightly, or wrongly, the Suffragettes celebrated their victory, and the movement largely came to an end. With no shared rallying cry, no consensus vision of where to go next, society started to find a new normal.

That new normal included women receiving higher levels of education than ever before, participating in the workforce in new ways, contributing to society, and living lives outside the home in addition to their work inside the home. In many ways, that dual-duty is not that different than what we experience in 2024 - but of course in 1924, your email didn't come home with you when you left work for the day.

Debate and discussion surely continued about the role and rights of women. Friedan herself does a masterful job linking the perceptions and views of women in society to Sigmund Freud, Carl Jung, and other psychologists sending theories into mainstream society. As newfound freedoms for women were being enjoyed, there was far from universal acceptance of this new societal structure - a situation that was ripe for the unrest that came next.

As World War II came to the United States, the work of men and women were about as different as could be, while at the same time suddenly overlapping at the margins. Then, in jaw dropping numbers, American men were sent overseas to fight and win the war, work that women were not generally able to participate in. Instead, they stepped into the void of many of the working roles that had previously been largely reserved for men.

It's difficult for us to imagine today. Our current societal structure engages in war (or war-like activities) with no perception of individual sacrifice toward the effort. The impacts of war are kept far away from individuals not actively engaging in it. As reference, when we launched a global war on terror, we were told all that was needed of us back home was to go to the mall. But it was different in the 1940s. Entire production lines were changed to produce more weapons, bullets, tanks, and vests. Supply chains changed quickly, ensuring maximum efficiency in warmaking. People back home took on new roles to help. Whether you were fighting on the front lines or still living in your town of 1,500 people (now 1,000 people), *you had a role to play.*

Everything you could imagine was rebranded to be part of a cause greater than yourself. What always comes to mind for many people is images of Rosie the Riveter. A strong, powerful, capable, feminine woman stepping in to do "man's work" while our boys were overseas defeating fascism. It wasn't just Rosie, though. There was an endless stream of propaganda from the United States government about the small efforts we make at home for the greater good. Think of "Victory Gardens" - a concept put forward on posters designed to rebrand the growing of backyard tomatoes and carrots as part of the effort to beat back evil in the world. If you were growing and using your own rhubarb, you weren't just engaging in a hobby or saving on your grocery bill, you were alleviating a little bit of pressure on the food supply so that we could better prosecute the war overseas.

So much of daily life was viewed through the lens of how it impacted the cause that we were all fighting. The universal focus of the power of individual impact was much more successful in the 1940s than would be today. Take for example the efforts to draw a connection between individual choices and climate change. In today's world, we receive messages about the carbon footprint of our plate, we are challenged to question plastic straws (but not the cups!), or the need to embrace alternative sources of energy. So, it's easy to imagine the messaging - but it's clear that the American public responded much more readily in World War II than we would today. To verify that for yourself, offer someone a paper straw for their iced latte.

As World War II raged on, women were doing an enormous amount of work carrying their share of the war effort. In doing so, everything they did was given a new sense of purpose and meaning, regardless of their income, education level, number of children, or work outside the home. They were made to feel like they were contributing to something bigger than themselves.

Spoiler alert: we won that war. The boys returned home, although many stayed on the coasts, preferring the community of men they formed away from their hometowns. Most came back to their communities and attempted to start new lives. A grateful nation (as the story is told) delivered the GI Bill, among other social programs, to help reintegrate them into society. This led to an absolute explosion in the American middle class and new families moving out to the suburbs.

For reasons that are deeply varied, many women made the choice to leave their professional paths and "return home." This phrasing works, even for women who never led a home before - instead - there was a collective action of a subset of women making the same choice at the same time. Friedan's work examines the social and cultural causes leading to that choice, but for the sake of this discussion, what needs to be understood is that there were cultural cues sending women back into the home. No doubt, these women believed they were continuing to fulfill their role in society, destined for a happy, comfortable existence.

Except, they didn't.

World War II didn't *cause* the problem with no name. Instead, it is best viewed as the incendiary incident. Without it, *The Feminine Mystique* would have taken a much different shape. Friedan recounts an endless number of women describing their "Occupation: Housewife" existence as numbing, monotonous, unfulfilling, and depressing. We can best understand the experience of our grandmothers not in isolation of this particular time, but with the broader context of the years preceding it.

In 2017 (based on the memory of the author), the Wisconsin Association for College Admission Counseling held its annual conference, with a keynote speaker discussing generational change. The refrain from the presentation did so well in explaining human behavior - at least in the context of generational change. "Every generation takes for granted the good and rebels against the bad." It's this mindset that explains how Americans elected Bill Clinton, then George Bush, then Barack Obama, then Donald Trump, then Joe Biden. With each transition, it's as though voters went looking for someone as opposite from their predecessor as is possible.

That's how to understand the decision women made when they chose to become 1950s suburban housewives. Remember, they had lives, goals, ambitions, and direction before they made that choice. Sure, for some, even as young girls, "occupation: housewife" may have always been their ultimate goal. For many others, this meant abandoning their own professional ambitions. Friedan shares the experience of talking with seniors at Smith College, about to earn their degree. Some of these women had jobs lined up, others had future husbands already waiting. The competing perspectives on which was better is a fascinating read within the broader context of *The Feminine Mystique*, but it also underscores the point - not everyone who became a 1950s suburban housewife did so out of necessity. At the same time, their decision to do so was not always enthusiastic.

Much like the generational speaker at the WACAC conference suggested, they were taking for granted the good of the generation before them - the freedom to make choices, access to education, the ability to enter the workforce, or to choose not to. Then, they rebelled against the bad - the inherent stress that comes from working while there is an unequal division of labor at home. The sense of guilt for not being able (or willing) to spend every moment doting over your children. The judgment that comes from peers (or worse, in-laws!) for prioritizing yourself over your children.

If they had just made that choice, take for granted the good and rebel against the bad, I am not convinced Betty Friedan would have tapped into such a strong reservoir of "something is wrong" as she did when she set about writing *The Feminine Mystique*. Prior to that, a woman who worked as a housewife did not have the experience of feeling like her garden was meaningful, that her work had a purpose.

During the war, they had it, that sense of purpose. Even if "they" does not apply to every individual woman - collectively - they had it. A recognized "life of meaning" for one was a life of meaning for the group overall.

The problem that has no name was not just about the absence of purpose and meaning. If it is, we would rightly blame World War II and the societal restructuring that came after as the cause. That would be an attribution error. Instead, the experience of purpose *during* World War II exposed the lack of purpose *before and after*. It was the sudden absence of purpose and meaning that caused 1950s suburban housewives to critically examine their role in society in a new way.

A newfound monotony, that is not helping to defeat Hitler.

A drowsy list of mundane tasks, that is not saving the world from Mussolini.

A sense that tomorrow holds no new possibilities than today, while also not pushing back against Hirohito.

They had all of that.

It was taken away.

COVID-19

Much like World War II had an incendiary impact on women who opted to become 1950s suburban housewives after the war, so too did COVID-19 impact people who became admissions counselors in 2022 and beyond. This reality is one of the reasons the staff morale crisis that started during the pandemic has been so intractable.

Plainly, if COVID-19 hadn't happened, *The Admissions Counselor Malaise* would have remained dormant. There would not have been an acute staff morale crisis after the pandemic which remains a pulsing struggle to this day. Of course, the underlying problems were there, but we had come to accept them. Much like the fish doesn't know how to think about water, admissions counselors considered the environment we were all operating in as unchangeable.

Until we quickly changed everything for COVID-19, demonstrating that yes, everything was changeable if there was a need. And indeed, there is a need. Of course, the definition of the word "need" is doing a lot of work. What we collectively learned is that when there is an *institutional need*, in this case the continued thirst for revenue and enrollment throughout the pandemic, there is literally nothing we have ever done that can't be undone, remade, or created anew.

Nothing.

There was nothing sacred. Nothing untouchable. We were not held back by "the way things have always been." The typical excuses preventing change on a college campus were washed away, and suddenly, creative solutions were allowed to thrive. Counselors had a voice in how they did their work, proving that they could maintain and build relationships from anywhere there was an internet connection.

The realization that anything could change when there was an institutional need caused admissions counselors to ask a reasonable question: can we make other changes when there is a student need, or a staff need? Of course, the answer has been a firm "no" from most campus administrations. This brought into stark relief the reality that we hadn't fully accepted or recognized: an institutional demand for revenue has fully pushed the needs of the student and the needs of the faculty and staff to the side.

COVID-19 allowed counselors to see through those statements as vapid rationalizations that are as insincere as they are inaccurate.

If institutions cared about their staff or their students as much as institutions care about revenue realizations, our jobs would look different. But our jobs don't look different, because institutions don't care about their staff or their students as much as they care about revenue. When there is an individual or collective need for change, whether it is for students or staff, the institutions clam up with responses of shared governance, competitive analysis, or even the mission-driven gaslighting of "it's really all about the students."

To fully understand COVID-19 as an incendiary incident, we need to explore the changes to our profession over the course of a generation. Just like the decision for 1950s suburban housewives to return to the home cannot be understood without taking stock of the decades before, so true is the understanding of how our profession has developed to its current form. While change is always happening, the starting point for this journey will be the very early 2000s.

Reviewing contemporary discussions of admissions at the time reveals that our focus was on commercialization. Enter *College Unranked,* a series of essays written by enrollment leaders, edited by Lloyd Thacker. Taken collectively, these pieces serve as an underpinning of an ethical battle happening on college campuses. Reviewing this text suggests that this was a moment where we were mainstreaming the shift to thinking of students as customers. This mindset shift introduced the concept of gift aid to students who don't need it (at the expense of those who do), a drive for ratings prestige motivating decisions more than the student experience, the commodification of higher education, and the corporatization of The College Board.

Re-reading this book as a historical document from our profession is equal parts fascinating and depressing. On one hand, the reader can so clearly see the moral viewpoint that the college is a social good, admissions professionals are educators, and that we need to hold the line against college leadership and the unquenching thirst for "more" - no matter the sacrifice. On the other hand, we have so clearly lost most of these battles over the last twenty years.

After all, the institutional will is strong, and it will sooner replace the people who object before changing its priorities.

Yet, there was no point where we waved the flag and declared defeat. Perhaps the adjustment to NACAC's SPGP explicitly endorsing per-student commission for some students was a watershed moment, or the later abandonment of the document overall. But for the most part, we lost through an unending series of colleges embracing commercialism through small steps. Like when we all signed up to send the same search letters from the same search company. Or when we all agreed that providing financial aid to the wealthy was actually a way to provide access to students we began gapping. While we never gave up on the idea of admissions counselors as educators, very few informed observers could reasonably describe us that way now.

If we could time warp to the 2004 NACAC Conference in Wisconsin and explain how we do our work, would they even recognize us as non-profit institutions of higher education? How long would it take for them to ask about SPGP?

No, we lost in a battle of inches - ceding ground, territory, and moral authority, one micro-decision at a time.

Because the loss of our core identity was so slow, we never updated it. At no point between the publishing of *College Unranked* in 2004 and today did we formally recognize the shift and make the appropriate changes. Instead, we continued to hire people attracted to a profession that no longer exists - one where the needs of students are primary. One where the drive for "more" is secondary. One where annual enrollment targets cannot be compared to quarterly profit targets at for-profit corporations.

This slow shift created an ever growing, slowly accumulating pile of uncomfortable rationalizations.

Every time a counselor was asked to continue recruiting a student despite an unconscionable gap or loan burden, the discomfort was amplified.

Every time we had to make the argument that giving wealthy families unneeded financial aid is how we can support more lower income students; the discomfort was amplified.

Every time we had to put in effort to grow an applicant pool ever larger, instead of working well with the students already interested in us, the discomfort was amplified.

So, when COVID-19 washed away the tired excuses that prevented change and progress that college leadership had used as a shield for decades, counselors came back to the office with a long list of changes.

Institutions could have come back from the pandemic in a golden era of staff morale. We had all learned that rapid change and adoption was possible. We could have come back to campus and initiated sincere conversations with students, staff, and faculty, about what else we need to change about the campus to improve. We could have taken the lessons from the emergency of COVID-19 and applied them to long-simmering issues of discontent and frustration.

Instead, college leadership determined that everyone needed to quickly "go back to normal" - and anyone complaining or raising frustration must be the problem. Facing a chorus of angst among campus faculty and staff, campus leadership responded with "nobody wants to work anymore."

COVID-19 didn't cause the frustration with admissions counselors. It revealed that the long-simmering frustrations could be resolved after all, if only the institution wanted to.

The ability to change quickly was there.

Then, it was taken away.

TEEGE METTILLE

IDLE HANDS

If the incendiary incident of COVID-19 helped college admissions professionals see how their job has changed, it also helped them see how their work had grown to levels that are both unmanageable and unsustainable - at least if we are to maintain deep connections with the students we work with. The ever-growing applicant pool is one of the root causes of The Admissions Counselor Malaise, and it is a cause of our own making.

The simple fact is that college admissions leaders have regularly been approaching each new recruiting cycle with a goal of increasing applications. It's why a college being down in applications, unless being done intentionally, is such a red flag. As one of my mentors and guides in this profession, Jim Miller, once told me, "If you're not up about 5%, you're actually down."

Once we accept the idea that more applications is always the goal, colleges set about working relentlessly towards that - with no shortage of private corporations who promised each of us the applicant pool of our dreams. Of course, these promises never materialized, because on almost every college campus, the applicant pool of our dreams was always "more than we had last year."

Sure, we might have a desire to change the shape or tenor of the applicant pool, but that was always secondary to the first goal: we need more. Whether we looked at declining populations, declining yield, declining enrollments, or declining revenue, we simply set about getting more applications.

To be fair, when faced with increasing populations, we also set out to get more applications.

When we increased yield, we also set out to get more applications.

When enrollment increased, we also set out to get more applications.

When revenue was up, we also set out to get more applications.

No matter what happened, what our results were, whether we met our goals, exceeded our goals, or fell short of our goals, next year, we still tried to get more applications. We just came to accept the faulty proposition that however many applicants we balanced this year, we have capacity for a few even more next year.

For modern day admissions counselors, it can feel like a strange experience - this constant expansion of workload - each year, pressing against the limits of our work / life balance and the time constraints of reality. While this may indeed be a new situation for our professional staff, we are fortunate to be able to turn to another group of people who found a way to fill every available minute with just a bit more work.

Housework Is Never Done!

Remember, the 1950s suburban housewife wasn't a role that was the natural evolution of women over time - instead it was directly oppositional to the evolving mores after the ratification of the 19th amendment. What Friedan documented is that when women had the ability to lead careers and lives based on their own drive towards fulfillment, they managed to balance their personal pursuits with the needs and responsibilities around the home. They managed this even though it was far from a 50/50 partnership with their husband.

Yet somehow, the 1950s suburban housewife, without taking a job outside the home, managed to be more exhausted and shorter on time than women who were balancing other responsibilities. With fewer roles, they had a fuller calendar. This was a perplexing challenge facing mid-century society - it was simply inconceivable that time could function this way. Certainly, a woman in this situation who felt like there were not enough hours in the day could not get a sympathetic ear from someone who was currently working or previously had worked outside the home as well.

It turns out, as Friedan documented, that housework had a way of expanding to fill the available time. Because being a wife and a mother were the primary identity markers, and women were told to expect an overwhelming sense of satisfaction and fulfillment from that work, it became all consuming. In this impossible scenario, if a woman was able to complete her housework for the day in four hours and all her children were at school, *what was her purpose the rest of the time?*

So, there must not be "the rest of the time" - and the work of Occupation: Housewife expanded to fill every available minute of a woman's day. The tasks, while routinized, could easily become endless. For example, a housewife might spend hours scrubbing floors every Friday, to have the home as clean as possible for the weekend. However, it's easy to see how redoing this task on Monday could fill the week and avoid a moment of looking around with nothing productive to do. Of course, if that wasn't enough, why not do it again on Wednesday?

Collectively, this created a cultural standard of cleanliness that rose to absurdist levels. In conversations with my grandmother, who herself was a 1950s suburban housewife, one could find her using the phrase, "you could eat off of her floors." Which … ewww. But, in that phrase, you hear a few things. During this era, there was no such thing as "too clean." Second, whatever level of cleanliness you found in a home was "hers" - either a point of pride or embarrassment - either way, it was hers.

The scope expanded as well. The work of Occupation: Housewife was regularly expanding to encompass a broader range of tasks. As the vignette from *Roseanne* listed at the beginning of this book highlights, it was very easy for the work of a 1950s suburban housewife to expand further than we might have expected. This came to include managing finances, helping children with homework, even volunteering in local groups (if the floors are clean enough) for the benefit of the family's position in the community, of course.

Through her time as a 1950s suburban housewife, each individual woman was faced with incredibly challenging thoughts if their work ever came to be done. *Is this all?* As a proactive avoidance tactic, she found ways to make sure her work was never, ever done. No matter how clean, it could be cleaner. No matter how ironed the sheets are, they could be re-laundered. There was always another task, always another chore, always something else she could do to be a better wife and mother. At the end of each year, month, or even day, she could look back and say, "I can take on a bit more."

She could say that, only up until the moment that she herself broke.

Manifest Destiny

It's difficult to explain this constant increase in applications to folks who don't work in our profession. Of course, the idea of "more" is quick to get - but what people outside of the world of admissions sometimes miss is this sense of institutional entitlement. College Presidents and Boards are much like politicians and pop stars: they believe their own hype, even to their detriment.

Currently, across the country, there are a wide range of institutions. Sure, some have genuinely unique features, but most are (definitionally) within one standard deviation of the typical college. It's why a search company could make insane amounts of money sending the same message on different college letterheads and generate inquiries and applications - because much of what we say about our institution is not actually unique.

Yet most institutions do not have the self-awareness, the realistic picture of their role in the higher education marketplace, to understand what that means. Or if they do, perhaps they do not have the willingness to accept the implications.

No, because institutions are run by true believers, they have a genuine, albeit misguided, belief that the number of students they determine they need, *they deserve.* Not only that, but they also have a genuine, albeit misguided, belief that they should be able to enroll these students at the discount rate they determine they need, *they deserve.* Far too often, institutions aren't building goals and revenue models based on the world around them, they are doing it based on internal calculations, and then demanding that someone, anyone, make the world operate how the institution thinks it should.

Thus, the concept of Manifest Destiny applies so well to colleges and universities. There is nothing about our founding in 1776 that called for a coast-to-coast expansion - we just decided that it would. Similarly, there is nothing about an individual institution's existence that calls for the enrollment and discount numbers they want - they just decided that. However, much like Manifest Destiny drove territorial expansion decisions for generations, so too have our recruitment models been driven by unresearched goals and expectations that are disconnected from the world around us.

This has expressed itself in the constant drive to increase applications. Each year, virtually every college has a goal to get more applications.

This is true when enrollment is increasing, holding steady, or decreasing.

This is true when revenue is increasing, holding steady, or decreasing.

This is true when their target population is increasing, holding steady, or decreasing.

This is true when their marketing budget is increasing, holding steady, or decreasing.

This is true when their staffing levels are increasing, holding steady, or decreasing.

Colleges are consistently increasing applications, even though admissions leaders have come to clearly understand that the relationship between increased applications and increased enrollment is incredibly tenuous. Yet, we do it, and each year, we strive for more applications, because that's the one variable of this equation that we have the most control over:

Applications x Admit Rate x Yield Rate x Net Price = Revenue

The trends are not so simple and precise, but let's take the conventional wisdom of 5% - that you need to increase your applicant pool by 5% each year just to hold steady among colleges and universities. As the starting point, let's look at 2004, the year *College: Unranked*, edited by Lloyd Thacker was published by the Education Conservancy. If a counselor had a territory load of 250 admits in 2004, what does twenty years of 5% increases look like?

2004 - 250 admits

2005 - 263 admits

2006 - 276 admits

2007 - 289 admits

2008 - 304 admits

2009 - 319 admits

2010 - 335 admits

2011 - 352 admits

2012 - 369 admits

2013 - 388 admits

2014 - 407 admits

2015 - 428 admits

2016 - 449 admits

2017 - 471 admits

2018 - 495 admits

2019 - 520 admits

2020 - 546 admits

2021 - 573 admits

2022 - 602 admits

2023 - 632 admits

2024 - 663 admits

20 years later, the number of admitted students a counselor is expected to manage has grown 265%, thanks to the power of compounding increases. While compounding is your friend in your retirement account, it is not in your friend in your admit pool. Of course, these numbers presume an annual similarity which is not real, does not account for population changes (as the drive for more applications does not), and does not recognize years when the average applicant pool did not rise as fast or years when it rose much faster. The goal of this is not to document the trials and tribulations of one individual counselor in their role for 20 years, but instead to show how the annual choice to grow the applicant pool has impacted the workload.

For the sake of clarity, at this rate, the growth of this workload crosses over 300% in the year 2027, and 400% in 2033.

You might be asking, "why does this matter?" A consistent 5% increase, each year, for 20 years, accumulators to a 265% increase. Unless the number of admissions counselors on each college campus has increased by the same rate, we have created a scenario where a college somehow needs to juggle more applicants per counselor than we did a generation ago. Even with staff increases along the way, it simply is not possible for us to develop the same type of relationship with each student that we did in 2004.

In 2004, our profession was engaged in a conversation about commercialization of higher education. Voices like Thacker's were raising concerns that colleges were becoming a commodity, and we were losing the individuality of the student in the process. We collectively responded by loading on more and more applicants per counselor, one ladle at a time, over the course of a generation.

By growing the applicant pools, we have unintentionally and slowly changed the job away from what it was, to something we would not have created from scratch.

We turned the applicants themselves into a commodity.

TEEGE METTILLE

CALLING ALL CORPORATIONS

In post-industrial America, if there is a problem where profit can be made, there'll be a corporation with a solution at a "low, low price!" While some people will identify this as a feature of capitalism, at least the American variety - the profit-motive leading to new and creative problem solving, there is a darker side to it. Yes, the desire for profit can drive corporations to develop solutions, it can also drive corporations to develop problems, so that solutions for these newly created problems, can be sold.

For a low, low price, of course.

For both populations we are discussing, modern day admissions counselors and 1950s suburban housewives, corporations descended, both as the problem creator and the problem solver. Particularly "innovative" corporations found a way to monetize both sides of the coin. In both cases though, it is worth noting that the work of the corporations didn't just lead to exceeding quarterly stock expectations - it led to actual damage to the mental health and well-being of their victims.

Or customers - however you want to think about them.

In 2012, the NACAC conference was held in Denver, and one of the exhibitors had brought in a virtual reality skiing experience. Come engage with the company, leaving your contact information of course, and you could have your own virtual skiing moment added to the conference. To be honest, it seemed like a cool addition, and there certainly wasn't any downside.

However, a long-time admissions vice president vented about the commercialization of admissions. Exasperated, he pointed to this virtual reality machine as the perfect example, but just an example. "Look around this exhibit hall - look at all the money being spent here. Where did the money for all of this come from?"

Of course, the lesson to be taken away was that the money, ultimately, came from students who we professed to be serving by taking this trip to Denver, while hopping in a virtual reality capsule for our own mountain skiing adventure.

"Go through the sessions being offered. It used to be that a few of them had vendors - now most of them do!"

Those of us who haven't seen the profession transition over forty years could be forgiven for not immediately connecting with the problem. After all, these corporations are here to help, offering products, services, and solutions designed to help us better serve students. Why shouldn't they be leading sessions, hosting receptions, and even giving us a virtual reality experience?

That mindset, however, presumes that corporate America came in just when solutions were needed. A more thorough analysis points to a more troubling connection - many of these corporations created the problems they are now charging colleges (ultimately, students) to fix.

For a low, low price, of course.

The experience of 1950s suburban housewives followed a similar path. At the time, corporations identified that there was a problem in terms of how these women were relating to their role in society, *and that there was money to be made.*

It wasn't enough that the work of women expanded to fill the available time - now they needed to be made to feel that the solution to The Feminine Mystique could be purchased.

For a low, low price, of course.

The Complexification of Housework

There was a system my grandmother used to follow for ironing everything. There was a specific spray, a way she would sprinkle all clothing, rolling them for a set amount of time, before ultimately, mercifully, finally ironing them to be done with the job. Of course, built into this is one of the foundational aspects of The Feminine Mystique - the complexification of the work.

It wasn't just enough for women to feel and be busy, with never enough time to complete the growing list of tasks she would give herself. Simply having things to do did not give 1950s suburban housewives a sense of purpose and meaning in their work. They needed to not just be busy, they needed to be irreplaceable.

This is where corporations stepped in. There was a point in time where your cleaning products were relatively basic, and one solution really did clean most things. However, there are two problems with that simplistic approach: anyone could do it *and* it didn't leave much room for growth in quarterly profit margins. So, as outlined in Friedan's work, domestic labor became a new and profitable industry in America.

Suddenly, specialized cleaning products were filling shelves across America - and work was being done to educate 1950s suburban housewives on the different uses of each one. The same was true about ever more complicated machines designed to make their day easier - a washing machine with specific settings for specific items, a chest freezer that is different than a regular freezer, and vacuum cleaners with enough attachments to reach every single nook and cranny of your house. Fear not - if there was an area out of reach, there was a special extension you could buy to reach it.

For a low, low price, of course.

As the work of Occupation: Housewife became progressively more complicated, there became new problems that corporate America was uniquely positioned to solve. Of course, new chemicals, machines, attachments, detachments, services, and offerings would be made available to solve the problems *that these same corporations created.*

Yet, for the 1950s suburban housewife, this was an acceptable creation. If your twelve-year-old child can do your laundry just as effectively as you, how do you feel a sense of purpose and fulfillment in your work? Enter a washing machine that is just too complicated for your pre-teen, and suddenly, there's something that you *and only you* can do.

Then, the cycle begins again - the very machine that was designed, built, sold, and purchased, to make your life easier is now a time suck. You'll need to find another way to get more time back in your day. Perhaps with a different type of vacuum? The new broom? A type of window cleaner that doesn't leave streaks to be dealt with later. Who knows - but grocery stores, general stores, and department stores had no shortage of offerings, all designed to help 1950s suburban housewives out of the problem created for them.

For a low, low price.

Of course.

The CRM Data Creep

It is true that the work of being a 1950s suburban housewife is very different from the work of being an admissions counselor in 2024. However, the similarities continue to jump out. While housework expanded in multiple ways, so too has the workload of admissions counselors. As the workload expanded, the reliance on corporate solutions increased, creating a rinse-repeat cycle.

For admissions counselors, we needed more applications, and corporations jumped to the scene with solutions. Search letters, fast versions of your applications, social networking type websites generating inquiries, scraping inquiry forms from popular college websites, whatever a college was willing to pay for could be made available. These corporations were successful in generating new inquiries and applications, *but not necessarily interested inquiries and applicants.*

If the 5% year-over-year application growth had not coincided with a (mathematically unavoidable) decrease in yield, staffing levels could have increased. In fact, they would have increased across the campus, not just in the admissions office. But these new applicants weren't necessarily leading to new enrollments, and so we had a new problem: too many applicants.

What happened is easy to understand, but like much of what's changed in our profession, it occurred slowly. Very slowly. So slowly, in fact, we never made the necessary adjustments to the job or the people we hired to account for this new reality. The role of data management in a counselor's job has slowly evolved. What had once been only a minor aspect of their work is now, easily, the biggest portion of their job.

As we begin to walk through this slow evolution, there is a quote from the Wisconsin Association for College Admission Counseling conference in May, 2023, in Green Bay, Wisconsin that we should hold on to. In this particular breakout session, there was a panel of three recently retired admissions professionals, each a legend in their own right in our state. The conversation shifted to what changes, good or bad, they have noticed in our profession since they started. Perry Robinson, Past President of WACAC, retired school counselor (University School of Milwaukee) and Dean of Admissions (Denison University) summarized it the best. Quoting him directly:

> "You know, when I started in this profession, it was high-touch, low tech. Today, it has shifted, and it is now low-touch, high tech."

This one quote summarized so succinctly, so simplistically, what is one of the core components of *The Admissions Counselor Malaise*. Indeed, it's true - our profession used to be about building relationships with students, maybe relying on an archaic database or spreadsheet to develop an initial outreach list. From there, it was up to the connection between the humans in the process: admissions counselor, school counselor, student, and parents, to drive the ball down the field. This was before the era of emails, or even websites. To get information about a college, students had to interact with someone at the institution. That was the admissions counselor, who could not engage with fake personalization the way we can today, {{reader_name}}.

At no point did anyone choose to move away from that. Instead, we move through in stages, slowly evolving, step by step. First, websites came online in the mid-90s, becoming ubiquitous around 2000. These primitive websites were not responsive, engaging, or even clear who the main audience was: current or prospective students. Second, email became an option to engage at scale, and slowly became the primary outreach tool somewhere between 2005 and 2010, depending on your institution's uptake. In both of those cases though, the digital communication method was meant to be, and actually was, supplemental to the counselor / student relationship.

Looming in the distance, though, was the modern CRM, starting to build a backlog of data elements. What initially began as a way to measure the ROI on a specific source eventually expanded to include email open rates, then visit windows, then FAFSA position, then email clicks, then Zinch profile data, then raise.me totals, and more. Always more. There never stopped being more, even to this day. Each year, institutions relied a little bit more on the data warehouse, and a little less on the human relationships in the recruitment process.

At some point, somewhere between 2004 and 2024, the data warehouse overtook, and eventually consumed human relationships as the main driver in the recruitment process. Much like the ever-expanding list of chores for 1950s suburban housewives, CRM systems slowly took over our work.

As we walk through the unending expansion of the role of the CRM, hold these two questions in your mind:

1. What does this evolution mean for *who* we should be hiring as admissions counselors?
2. How does this reflect the sentiment from Perry Robinson in May, 2023, that this is now a high-tech, low-touch profession?

Of course, there has always been a set of data kept on students. If nothing else, their physical application form was stored in a file folder, with their name on it. A physical file, made from paper, that was stored in a large, metal box somewhere on a college campus. Sure, admissions counselors were expected to use the information contained in those archaic files, but there could never have been an assumption that the application file would tell you what you need to know to recruit a student. Instead, at best, it would give the admissions counselor a starting point to begin the relationship building process.

Somewhere along the way, this information started to be manually entered into spreadsheets that could be sorted or manipulated to help a counselor or director understand who was applying, what their majors of interest were, etc. From there, very basic databases came online, with a CRM-like interface developed, that expanded further the information we were collecting on students. Since most of these systems were homegrown, they were all limited by the imagination, use cases, and technical expertise of a specific institution.

Enter the modern CRM. When we think about the modern CRM, there are a few that came online about 20 years ago, give or take. Some have since fallen away or otherwise been merged into the surviving systems - but their roots go back to this time. It is here that the transition from single spreadsheets or basic databases to the modern CRM where our story gets interesting.

Spoiler alert: it leads to unhappy, unsatisfied admissions counselors - *The Admissions Counselor Malaise*.

Each institution embraced the age of the modern CRM on their own timeline. Most of us were there about ten years ago. Sure, there were and are some exceptions, and we all feel a bit of sadness for our peers still working without these tools into 2017, 2018, and beyond, but there's no way around it: the modern CRM found a market, took its foothold, and is now firmly ensconced in our work. Today, unlike years gone by, the tracking data we collect on students is not limited to the imagination, capacity, and needs of an individual institution - we are collectively growing our data warehouse. For example, once a CRM provider adds in the tracking of text message engagement, it usually makes that a feature across all of their partner institutions, whether they asked for it or not.

This is creating the (false) illusion that admissions offices can be on a level playing field with our corporate partners, who had been wowing us for years with their impressive analytics and other data tools. Think back to the data presentations you received from your vendors 15 years ago - how basic would they look compared to what you are able to do in your CRM today? But, if our search company could run analytics on yield rates based on how long it took to send the first email after the names were released, why can't we internally run those numbers for the speed at which we respond to a data import for an inquiry generation company?

For good or for bad, we have moved in this direction, and started to enthusiastically embrace the moniker of being "data driven" in our decisions. For many of us, we started to see that there were data secrets, or pearls of yield signals, tucked away deep within our CRM data lake. If only we could unlock them, read the data trails with the right decoder ring, our recruitment efforts would successfully roll up like the last few chapters of a Dan Brown novel - full of massive insights and a dramatic reveal, all hiding in plain sight all along.

This approach was spreading across our profession - it seemed every institution had a few folks who leaned more on the data than others. Those of us who took time away from student outreach in favor of data analysis were more novel, doing something different, and sometimes, finding a new insight to share with the team and earning respect from our peers. (This was true even when the flashy new insight we developed was nothing more than anecdata.) Those of us who did not lean into data analysis in our territories continued the never-ending task of reaching out to students individually to build relationships. Slowly, the informal reward system of college admissions shifted, and our professional ethos moved from personal connection to query development.

Just a little bit, each year. But as the 5% app growth compounding shows, a little bit each year amounts to a drastic change when given time to grow. The change builds and builds, ultimately creating the scenario we find ourselves in today - about a third of every hour a counselor is doing their work, their supervisors expect them to be in the CRM.

In the CRM, not on the phone with students.

In the CRM, not answering texts or emails.

In the CRM, not explaining financial aid packages.

In the CRM, not meeting with campus visitors.

The admissions leaders expect all those things to happen as well, but on balance, their expectation of each counselor is about 650 hours of CRM work, per year. This work includes reviewing CRM records, entering contacts, building queries, working in the spreadsheets that come out of the CRM, and more. Of course, no one would have picked that number (650 hours) if asked plainly. Instead, through a time study sponsored by enroll ml (which you can read about in the appendix) breaking down the individual work expectations of their team, the minutes add up to hours, adding up to 1/3 of a counselor's job.

Presuming you might be skeptical, answer just a portion of the enroll ml Time Work Study interview questions for yourself. Answer the questions in order. If you are an admissions leader, give your honest, genuine expectation. If you are an admissions counselor, do your best to answer what you believe to be the expectations your supervisor has of you. Here is the script:

> I presume that before reaching out to a student (either proactively or responding to a call/email/text), you want the counselor to review the CRM record of a student. (100% of the time, the answer was yes.)
>
> With that confirmed, let's work through this aspect of their work.
>
> 1. How much time does it take for a counselor to review the CRM and identify the major enrollment stages a student has worked through. Think things you would report to the board - FAFSA filing, documents received, visited campus, etc.
>
> _____ (Answer in seconds)
>
> 2. How much time does it take for a counselor to review the CRM and identify the non-major processes a student has worked through. Think things that you wouldn't report up - high school visit attendance, 7th semester transcripts, logging in to review their aid package, etc.

_____ (Answer in seconds)

3. Now think about how much time it would take for a counselor to review the CRM and identify the communication record so far. Things like email engagement, web sites visited, recorded calls from parents, etc.

_____ (Answer in seconds)

4. Now tell me, on average, how many students per day you expect your counselors to reach out to, again, proactively, or reactively.

_____

To get to a final total, simply add up the seconds, multiply by the number of students, and you get a per-day expectation of just this aspect in the CRM. The median answers tended to total about five minutes per record to review. Some were higher, some were lower. Some depended on which CRM they were using, some depended on how well built their CRM was - but 5 minutes was the consensus. To get to those five minutes, they thought it would take about a minute or less to look up a student record and identify the major stages - those tend to be surfaced on the student's dashboard. About 90 seconds to identify the smaller stages. And about 2 ½ minutes to review the communication record and synthesize all the information to come up with a plan of outreach.

Five minutes to review a student record doesn't sound like a lot - after all, we should use the data we have spent so much time, effort, and money collecting. That's especially true if we want to earn the "data driven" moniker that is the hottest fashion accessory at every NACAC conference. In fact, there's even a pin you can get from one of the vendors to prove your data-driven-ness. So yes, five minutes to review the CRM data before communicating with a student isn't a lot. But then, multiply that by the number of students a counselor should connect with.

There was a WIDE range in responses here, but the median was right around 25 students per day, including proactive calls, email outreaches, or responding to incoming messages or visits.

5 minutes x 25 students = 125 minutes per day

125 minutes per day x 5 days per week = 625 minutes per week

625 minutes per week x 50 working weeks per year = 31,250 minutes per year.

31,250 minutes = 520.8 hour s per year.

In that time, your counselor hasn't reviewed any of the actual application data - so add time if you'd expect the essay to be re-reviewed or the transcript re-assessed before an outreach or a campus visit. Additionally, all the information is being interpreted quickly by one person, with their own biases and limitations - so that's 520.8 hours per year of time reviewing CRM records, and the results are strife with human fallacy.

In 520 hours, we haven't built a single query.

In 520 hours, we haven't built a single outreach plan.

In 520 hours, we haven't built a single relationship.

To get from 520 to 650, remember that we also expect counselors to log all their activities and interactions, and to use queries to make meaningful groups of an applicant pool that is somehow going to be 5% larger again this year.

Enter the modern CRM's query function.

Because we keep increasing the applicant pool, utilizing CRM data isn't just an expectation from the admissions leader, it is a necessity for counselors to sort through their applicant pool. There are just plain too many students per counselor - and too many who have little interest in the institution. So, we have no choice but to find ways to narrow it down - a problem created by our corporate friends who promised us that by putting our logo on top of the search letter they're sending out, all our enrollment dreams can come true.

For a low, low price, of course.

Much like corporations found ways to complicate laundry detergent, so too have the modern CRMs. They have first created, then cracked open a data warehouse beyond what any admissions counselor could ever make meaningful use of. What had been a simple list: call everyone who hasn't submitted the FAFSA is now something different. These queries can include new features, new limiters, new data elements. Enhancements or complications, depending on your perspective.

If you give a list of all non-FAFSA filers to your counselors and ask them to churn through them, chances are, frankly, the list is likely to be too large - especially if you expect a 5-minute review of each record before they make a call. Of course, they're also going to be wasting an enormous amount of time calling students who didn't submit the FAFSA because they have no interest in enrolling at your institution.

So, we add a column. Just one little column, at first. Perhaps it is noting whether they've visited or not. In doing so, we can better target our efforts. But, since we have the data attached to their visit, shouldn't we also include the rating they gave the campus tour in the post-visit survey evaluation? Perhaps there's a difference in the type of visit, so add a column to determine if it was a group visit or an individual visit. Did they sit in on a class or meet with a coach? Let's add that as well. Of course, we probably shouldn't exclude people who couldn't visit campus yet, but otherwise engaged with us, so let's add in a column about whether or not students came to a high school visit or were scanned at a college fair. Maybe we should also drop in the distance from campus feature that is available as an export. While you're at it with high school visits, we know that some high schools are better than others - we should probably consider the student's high school to get the best list.

You see, we can, and do, go on and on and on when developing these queries. There is no end to the number of variables we could pull in, under the (false) illusion that we are making a meaningful difference in our list building. We probably are not, but much like the 1950s suburban housewife who recently upgraded her dish detergent to the hypoallergenic skin soft brand, we *feel* like we are.

The CRM data creep has been going on for twenty years and is showing no sign of slowing down. Each year, admissions counselors are being asked to do more and more of their work in front of a screen instead of in front of a student.

Parent data matters more to us than parent perspectives.

Imagine a time machine - going back to that 2004 NACAC Conference in Milwaukee. Imagine bringing those counselors forward twenty years - how much of our work would they be able to understand? How much would they be able to do, after we trained them? Two reasonable questions, sure. But there's a more pressing question - even more alarming. It's a question that highlights the self-inflicted nature of a contributing factor to *The Admissions Counselor Malaise.*

If we did use a time machine to bring counselors from 2004 into 2024, and dropped them in today's admissions office, how much of the work we do today would they *want* to do?

Chances are - not much. But here's the rub - today's admissions counselors feel the same way about some of the most time-consuming aspects of their work. The difference between a time-traveled admissions counselor coming to work in 2024 and a modern admissions counselor coming to work in 2024: only the time-travelers know that there once was a better way.

To be blunt, as it's evolved, *this job sucks.*

DESPERATELY SEEKING MEANING

A healthy tomato plant.

Creating this in your backyard would not just slightly offset your grocery budget or be the envy of your neighbor who doesn't have a green thumb or your mother-in-law who doubted your skills as a homemaker. No, for a period of time in American history, a healthy tomato plant was also *needed* to save the entire planet from the rule of a fascist dictator.

Why in the world was it necessary to rebrand backyard gardens during World War II, from a housewife hobby into "Victory Gardens" - an important and crucial component of the United States' war effort?

Because people have an innate and powerful need to feel as though they are part of something greater - that their work has purpose and meaning. The idea, as branded in Victory Gardens, that we are each contributing to a massive effort, in line with our personal ethics and values, is an unseen imperative in our lives.

Lacking meaning, we start to slowly unravel. If our work doesn't have a purpose *that is in line with our values,* we will disconnect from it, even if we go through the motions.

If you look closely, you'll see that this might explain the foundational elements of the concept of quiet quitting that washed over our society after the pandemic. The idea that going above and beyond, without recognition or reward, as a baseline expectation, was suddenly challenged by people across industries. In fact, quiet quitting glorified the idea of "just" showing up to work when scheduled, doing your work while there, and then not working once you were done for the day.

Obviously, management in industries that have come to rely on unpaid labor from the "above and beyond" mantra was aghast, and felt a need to push back on what was perceived to be a dangerous new idea.

Yet, it's not new at all.

The disengagement.

The disconnectedness.

When our work no longer has purpose or meaning in line with our values, we pull back.

It's natural.

This disenchantment is the fuel that is powering *The Admissions Counselor Malaise*. For too long, admissions leaders have disconnected the work counselors actually do from the reasons they show up to work.

The "what" we do and the "why" we do it are now worlds apart. But modern-day admissions counselors aren't the first group of people who have struggled to come to terms with purposeless work.

Is This All?

Early in her book, Friedan shares the account of a 1950s suburban housewife who discussed the drudgery of her work as Occupation: Housewife.

- She wakes up early
- Prepares breakfast for the entire family
- Sees the older kids off to school and washes the dishes
- She then takes on household cleaning tasks such as:
  - Waxing the floors on Tuesdays and Fridays
  - Washing and ironing sheets on Wednesdays
  - Separating, drying, and folding laundry on Mondays and Thursdays

All of this, of course, while managing to entertain and educate the kids that are too young to go to school.

- Of course, they will need a mid-morning snack
- Then lunch, and more dishes
- She will put the kids down to an afternoon nap to work on:
  - the windows
  - the blinds
  - the carpet
  - the removable oven door
  - Or whatever the day calls for

Or, as we discussed in the *Idle Hands* chapter, whatever the day allows for. She will be hard at work preparing a large meal that is nutritious, healthy, tasty, and likely, messy - so that it is ready by the time her husband comes home from work.

Of course, during all of that, she sees the older kids home from school and discusses their day and helps with the homework.

She serves the meal, then washes the dishes again.

The evening calls for family time, perhaps an hour around the family television set, before beginning the bedtime routine, reading stories, putting kids to sleep.

At the end of the day, whichever day this happens to be, this particular housewife would collapse into bed, simultaneously feeling exhausted *and like she accomplished nothing at all.* As she looks ahead to her day tomorrow, where she would need to repeat every step of this over again, she sees another day of repetitive, monotonous drudgery.

She stares at the ceiling and asks herself, "is this all?"

Indeed, what is unpacked by *The Feminine Mystique* is that yes, indeed, that was all. In the post-war world built for (and by) these women, there was nothing more than that.

This was what they chose.

In this environment, she was told that the joy of raising her children and supporting her husband would give her the satisfaction of being a housewife and mother.

She was told that there was purpose and meaning in the work that she did - far more than if she was going to work every day.

She was even gaslit into believing that she alone carried special skills needed to complete her work. Imagine, she was told, if you needed to hire someone to run your household! They would need skills in accounting, chemistry (for cleaning chemicals), nutrition, education, and entertaining, just to get started! The "cost" of this labor was calculated, not to give these women any form of payment, but to pat them on the head to celebrate their financial contribution to the family by making no financial contribution at all.

So, each night, when a 1950s suburban housewife looked ahead to the next day, she came to see that yes, indeed, this was all. For as many tomorrows as she could foresee, this was all. This led to all sorts of challenging dynamics. Friedan lays out many of the personal and social challenges that came from 1950s suburban housewives returning to the home after the women before them won freedoms and possibilities that were not previously available. The number of women going to college skyrocketed, while the number of women working plummeted. There was a significant mismatch between the work assigned to these women and the skills, capacities, and abilities they brought to bear.

Women who could have gone on to careers in an industry they felt drawn to instead chose to stay at home, raising a family, expecting to feel personal fulfillment. She did not. One of the clearest reasons she did not is because the benefit she was bringing to society did not match her personal "why" - the reason she would want to get up in the morning and go to work.

Of course, there are women for whom the role of Occupation: Housewife was rewarding and fulfilling. There are any number of roles in society which are enriching and fulfilling for some people, but not others. Being a housewife was one of those roles - it worked for a few, but for many others, it felt like an unending trap. This is reflected in the rising rates of depression and suicide among women who were caught in it.

There is no evidence to believe that the work of being a 1950s suburban housewife brought inherent danger - no clear link to housework and depression. Instead, Friedan identifies a confounding variable - the lack of purpose. When a woman did not find personal value in the work she was doing, that it didn't just feel like a trap but was a trap, the lack of fulfillment became intensely problematic.

Of course, for women experiencing The Feminine Mystique, the impacts were severe. They were made to feel guilty if they wanted more out of life than raising their children. If living vicariously through the success of their children wasn't going to be enough for them, did that mean they were a bad mother? They were made to feel selfish and greedy if they wanted to engage in work outside the home. Of course, many women were taking on part-time work to contribute to the household or to get out of the house, but any time an incident arose with one of the children that she wasn't available for, the woman would feel (and probably was) harshly judged.

For most of these women, they continued in the drudgery, hoping against hope it would go away. But it wouldn't. Rates of alcoholism rose, as did the rates of tranquilizer prescriptions. Many women came to resent their children as the reason she gave up her personal ambitions and goals. Other women linked themselves so closely to their children that the children lacked independence and adult abilities as they grew up. Friedan outlined a situation that could easily have been labeled as the origin of helicopter parents.

By and large, when this disconnect between a woman's personal drive and the work of a 1950s suburban housewife came up, she would check out.

Net Tuition Revenue Goals

Let me say as plainly as I can:

Admissions counselors do not care about net tuition revenue goals.

Admissions counselors do not care about the institution's budget needs.

Admissions counselors do not care about improving the yield rate.

Sure, they are aware of these institutional goals and objectives, and will work to help achieve them. But they are the *institution's* goals, not the counselor's. Using the phrase "they do not care" is not to imply that they will just disregard these goals. They understand the concepts, they will engage with their director about them, and they will make the forward progress necessary to help achieve them. But *care*? No.

Admissions counselors *care* about providing access to higher education.

Admissions counselors *care* about the amounts of student loan debt being loaded on to the students they work with.

Admissions counselors *care* about how their work can help students find their fit.

The things that admissions counselors *care* about are the activities and goals that give their work purpose and meaning. When they love their institution - and they usually do when they start in the job - they want to help all students who would benefit from attending find their way to doing so. If it means talking with a student later at night than they'd like to because they are in a different time zone or even country, they'll do it. If it means finding time to squeeze in one more coffee shop interview between two college fairs, they'll do it. If it means working through a financial aid package yet one more time with parents to ensure they understand, they'll do it.

Admissions counselors care so much about access, student loan debt, and fit, that there is no amount of "above and beyond" that they won't go to be helpful.

At the same time, while they understand the importance of net tuition revenue, institutional budgets, and yield rate, there is no amount of "above and beyond" that they won't be resentful of, if those are the goals they are being asked to drive towards. In fact, when asked to put in the extra effort to increase the yield rate, it should be no surprise that an admissions counselor would embrace the concept of quiet quitting.

What is most vexing to admissions directors is the novelty of this concept being applied to our work. While there have always been varying levels of engagement and effort, the current state, where there is almost a wholesale pulling back, is difficult to understand. At a time when admissions directors have a deeper understanding of the impact of net tuition revenue, discount rate, and budget goals than ever before, why is it that admissions counselors are pulling back just when we need them the most?

The before- and post-covid focus of admissions leaders underwent an unperceived shift in focus. To be sure, the choice of the word unperceived is intentional. The shift is not imperceptible - it has just largely gone unrecognized. During COVID-19, many institutions saw very real, genuine threats to their ongoing viability. Without being able to know how long the pandemic would go on, what the impact would be to housing revenue, the added expenses of online education, the changes to retention rates that would be coming - everything was up in the air. The importance of revenue from new students, *any students,* was of paramount importance.

Prior to the pandemic, the most likely scenario was that the Vice President of Enrollment would be tasked with delivering to the Admissions Director the enrollment goals and the importance of them. These vice presidents served as a buffer from the vulture-like need for revenue (as described by Eric Hoover in September 2014) and the mission-driven admissions team. During the pandemic, both because of the ease of including more and more people on zoom meetings and because Presidents wanted to personally deliver the sense of urgency, admissions directors were brought into more of these conversations and included in discussions that they hadn't before. This is not suggesting a seismic shift - but a real one, nonetheless.

Either way, Admissions Directors came out of COVID-19 with a deeper commitment to doing their part to help the institution meet revenue goals. To find enough students, any students, to feed the financial beast - and less of an emphasis on the issues of access, student loan debt, and fit.

There's an incredibly simple example: test optional admissions. It is well established that the test optional movement was built for forty years, pioneered by Bates College. Becoming test optional was viewed as a way to increase access to higher education, because you could admit students (go ahead and read between the lines here) who you otherwise wouldn't admit (we all know what this means, right?) without negatively impacting the rankings (there it is) and thereby the prestige of the institution. Even with that secondary motivation, most of the time an institution would go through the process of becoming test optional by loudly trumpeting it as a move rooted in their commitment to access.

Then, COVID-19 hit, and we all had to shift. In Wisconsin, the massive wave of school closures began just before the statewide administration of the ACT. Any institution that required enough students from Wisconsin to enroll their class had no choice but to drop the test score requirement. So most of us did, quickly, with no research, no internal analysis of how the test scores impacted ongoing success, and no plan to more heavily weight other factors. It was just lobbed off the admissions application, with a battle ax, not a scalpel.

Has this move provided access? Yes.

Has this move helped enrollment? Yes. Or at least, it prevented a loss of enrollment.

Was this move pitched to counselors as being motivated by access? No.

So here we have a situation where colleges quickly moved en masse in deciding what many admissions counselors in 2018 would have celebrated: becoming test optional, increasing access, reducing the impact of a barrier that is felt differently by different populations.

Yet, the unperceived difference is significant. Admissions counselors saw firsthand that their institutions kept the testing requirements every year they could, even though it negatively impacted students. However, the moment it appeared that it would hurt the institution's revenue goals, they quickly dropped the testing requirement, most of them for good.

The message was clear: if it helps students, we'll think about it slowly and cautiously. If it helps us make money, we can and will move with expediency.

The argument here is not that institutions should not have gone test optional - they should have. They should have done it long before COVID-19, but that's an argument for another day. In fact, they should probably just go test blind, but again, that's another book altogether. The rapid adoption of test optional admissions was necessary given the drastic change in the admissions landscape. The argument here is simply that the motivation for the change does not line up with what drives an admissions counselor to pour effort into their work like we used to see from them.

The same story plays out similarly on campuses all over the country, for decisions small and large. Seeing the success of a massive policy win using the imperative of meeting institutional revenue goals, admissions leaders would be smart to use that rationale for any number of other initiatives.

Why do we need a full-tuition scholarship competition? It will help us meet revenue goals.

Why do we need a third admitted student day? It will help us meet revenue goals.

Why do we need faculty presence on a visit day? It will help us meet revenue goals.

Admissions leaders are now talking about their work in terms of net revenue, yield rates, and budget goals in a way that is a bit different than it had been before the pandemic. Not seismically different. Not drastically different. Not "is this the same job?" different. Admissions directors always knew and understood the importance of revenue to the institution. However, coming out of COVID-19, we moved a few ticks on the spectrum towards institutional goals, and in doing so, we've crossed over to a point where the connection between "why" we make our decisions as admissions leaders and "why" a counselor is committed to their work is strained.

Strained, stretched, and stressed. But not broken.

We can hold on to the connection between our work and institutional goals without alienating the lifeblood of our operation: the goodwill and commitment of admissions counselors. We can align the work that will help us achieve our institutional revenue objectives and fit the personal motivations and ethics of our admissions counselors.

But we must do so with intentionality.

VANISHING SUPPORT SYSTEMS

There are two types of rookie admissions counselors: those that go out with other counselors to the bar after a late-night fair, and those that go back to their room. For some, the end of a long day of high school visits, travel, and college fair engagement represents a moment of exhaustion. For others, it leaves them amped up, ready to continue connecting with their peers, sharing stories from the day, and developing a professional support network.

In some ways, introverts who retreated to their room missed out on an opportunity. Their extroverted counterparts found these nights out incredibly helpful, personally and professionally. They weren't just about drinks and music, although there was plenty of both, they were about making and managing meaningful connections and mentoring relationships with colleagues from other institutions. Professionals who understood our work, maybe even knew some of the people at our institution but were neutral enough to help us talk through some of the workplace challenges we were experiencing.

Sure, there were other ways to form this professional network. Just as effective, albeit much geekier, was the route many of us took: joining committees in our affiliate ACAC or ACRAO. For many of us, it is where we became involved for the first time with peers from other institutions, working together on problems, challenges, or opportunities that spoke to us beyond the individual needs and goals of our institutions. Here, many of us found colleagues who could understand our challenges and talk through them, without a DJ or bartender being present. Of course, this is in addition to the work of determining which color badges to use for exhibitors at the upcoming state conference.

These professional networks served a vital role in supporting each other. When a young professional is experiencing frustration in their work, sitting alone and stewing on it is dangerous. At the same time, discussing your frustrations at work with colleagues on campus may also not be smartest choice. So, these external colleagues have historically played a critical role in keeping frustrations in check and below a boiling point.

Then, with a cough, they were gone.

The Gaslighting

The term gaslighting is used regularly in everyday conversation, but its source is not always fully understood. In 1944, a movie titled *Gaslight* featured an intriguing plot: a man drove his wife to insanity by slowly convincing her that she couldn't trust her own perception, that she couldn't believe what her lying eyes were telling her. The specific example that created the term is turning on the exterior light (a gas flame) at times it shouldn't be on. When she asked about it, he would tell her that the gas light wasn't on. Together, they would go look, and he would have already turned it off, causing her to question if she really did see what she thought she had seen. Therein, we have the first known victim of gaslighting, in this case, a fictional character from a World War II era movie.

The 1950s suburban housewives were gaslighting each other all the time. Perhaps they were inspired by the movie? Earlier in this book, the concept that women would "perform happiness" for each other was discussed. This is one of the ways society was gaslighting individual women. In a world where rates of alcoholism, depression, and suicide were rising drastically among this population, everywhere they looked, their peers seemed to be happy and satisfied with their lot in life. Everyone, it seemed, *except them.* In publishing *The Feminine Mystique,* Friedan broke into the mainstream to destroy the facade, which may be the most important contribution the book made to the women of 1960s America.

Because these women were gaslighting each other by performing happiness, it became difficult to find a support network to discuss this problem that has no name. Remember the scene from *Roseanne* at the start of this book? There's a key moment - Roseanne (the character) has hit her breaking point, eventually telling Jackie, "I'm just not happy!" Then, as Roseanne covers her mouth, as if trying to put the words back, dramatic music begins, and Jackie seals off the room. After all the blinds are drawn and the doors are closed, she subversively tells Roseanne, "You are not alone. There are other women who feel the way you do!" While this is obviously a humorous and fictional portrayal, it is included in this text because it showcases the sense of trapped desperation and perceived isolation these women felt at the time.

They were left alone in their home, convinced they were feeling something that no one else would understand.

Of course, family was not helpful, either. A woman's husband was more likely to believe she was living a charmed existence than going through an existential crisis. After all, everywhere he looked in society, he received the message that the suburban home he was providing his family was exactly what he should be doing. The children in the home didn't know a world different from one where their mother appeared to be a happy homemaker - they couldn't be relied upon as an intergenerational support system.

Then, the in-laws, who were perhaps the most severe gaslighters in this whole scenario. My own grandma still enjoys telling a story from her first few years as a 1950s suburban housewife. Her mother-in-law was once very critical of cake mixes, specifically any that my grandmother used to bake for my grandfather. "You kids today don't appreciate the value of hard work!" she would lecture. One evening, while having dinner at her in-laws, she went to throw something away, and much to her shock, she saw the package of a cake mix - the very German chocolate cake served that night had come from a mix!

That incident happened more than 50 years ago - and my grandma still lights up when telling the story. That's how much of an impression that moment left, in large part because of the gaslighting that preceded it. The takeaway from this story is that everyone involved was in on the game - that a woman should be satisfied just knowing that she is creating a happy home for her husband and children. When you didn't feel that way, there was nowhere to turn. There was no support network you could confidently turn to get out of your own head as you spun through any frustrations you were experiencing over and over and over again.

Alone In a Zoom

COVID-19 took a lot of things from a lot of people - and for the purposes of this book, it's important to note that it took from counselors their external support network. As if losing access to this support network wasn't problematic enough, it happened right at the time that workplace stresses were hitting new levels. Instead of being able to connect with colleagues on the road to vent, get advice, or just think through a challenge, they found themselves alone, trying to make sense of a suddenly changed world.

The new causes of the stress were significant.

Depending on when a college closed its admissions office to visitors, and when it opened back up, counselors could have felt a very reasonable concern for their own physical health. Remember, these decisions were being made long before vaccines were available and treatment options were as effective as they had become. Many of us rightly believed that a diagnosis of COVID-19 could have fatal consequences.

While that stress weighed on everyone, before federal relief programs were announced, institutional survival was also a real threat. Institutions became desperate for revenue in ways we could not have predicted. Most colleges sent students away around spring break and made the difficult decision to refund housing costs. Of course, the housing *expenses* weren't gone - and so a very significant mid-cycle budget shift hit institutions unexpectedly, right during yield season for the fall 2020 class. The sense of urgency and desperation to do *whatever it took* to get students to enroll landed in a consistent, across-the-board way our profession hasn't seen.

Every outreach method was transitioned to a virtual offering as quickly as possible. It goes without saying, the rapid transition did not mean every zoom visit was good. However, whether the virtual visit day was good or not did not change the amount of work it took to pull off. The thought, challenge, and creativity from a counseling team making this up in real time was a new addition to the yield cycle. The mental energy that it took to create that first round of zoom events for admitted students is far beyond the mental energy it would have taken to once again hold a version of the admitted students day your institution had been doing for years. Throw in the institution's desperate need for the events to succeed, and it's easy to see how counselor stress exceeded previous boundaries.

Co-workers, supervisors, Presidents, student workers - everyone was at their absolute limit. In fact, most of us were operating for weeks at a level of stress beyond what we would have thought was possible in 2019. At the time, it seemed like our entire society was functioning with the shortest of fuses, ready to be lit with the slightest inconvenience or provocation. Team members who would normally be calm, understanding, and patient were less likely to be so admirably reasonable. Having to do their job in brand new ways, while the stakes were so much higher, all while having to stay home and fight for space with children around the dining room table to take a zoom staff meeting was just too much.

Students were shell shocked and didn't know how they were supposed to react. Remember, we didn't automatically close campuses for the year - we closed them for two weeks, one of which was usually spring break. You may remember Vice President Mike Pence standing in front of a sign that read "two weeks to crush the curve" which came to be replaced by a sign that read "thirty days to crush the curve" before ultimately getting rid of a time frame. Students had to make their enrollment decisions without the ability to attend the admitted student days they had been expecting to.

Deposit deadlines extended - stretching out this brutal yield season for another month.

Another month of shell-shocked students.

Another month of surprisingly short-fused co-workers.

Another month of more zoom programs.

Another month of an institutional hunger for revenue that carried us into June.

During all of this, who could these counselors turn to for support, for venting, for perspective, and for problem solving? Certainly, the idea of another zoom meeting between co-workers on campus was not going to carry much appeal. Even if it were, as has been discussed, there's a limit to how much someone will (or should) vent to a colleague on campus versus an external contact. Support from home was probably lacking as well - everyone there was reeling from the changes washing over us as well.

The spring college fair circuit was cut short, and that had measurable impacts on inquiry numbers. Yet it's damage to counselor support networks that has had the longest-term impact on our profession. Certainly, we could have made it through the spring disruption if the fall travel season had come together. But it didn't. The relationships counselors had with fellow road warriors atrophied and just weren't accessible for two years.

Two years where counselors would take their frustrations at work and process them internally, even if they were external processors.

Two years where counselors would not realize that some challenges are universal, and not unique to their institution, so they could act accordingly.

Two years where counselors would need to rely on themselves and remind themselves about the value they are bringing to students in spite of the frustrations they feel in their offices.

The lost support network has been a contributing factor to *The Admissions Counselor Malaise*. Now that the college fair circuit is back in place, we cannot assume that these support systems will serve the same purpose they did before. Like every other aspect of society that changed during the pandemic, it broke. If it is to be put back together the way it was, it will require a new level of intentionality to make that happen.

THE POWER OF PERSONAL CONNECTION

Throughout this book, we have touched back to the experience of 1950s suburban housewives to draw inferences and understanding to the experience of admissions counselors in 2024. However, as with each attempt to build on the work of academic giants whose shoulders we stand upon, there comes a time where we must take a step beyond the path laid out before us.

We come to that moment now - the final (and perhaps most impactful) cause of *The Admissions Counselors Malaise*. It is not part of the experience identified by Betty Friedan for 1950s suburban housewives.

Instead, we now must lean on our peers, colleagues, friends, and families from different corners of campuses, different sides of the desk, indeed, different industries altogether, to understand how admissions counselors are processing their relationship to work post-pandemic.

As has been identified in The Chronicle of Higher Education and Inside Higher Ed, the turnover crisis is real all over campus, but particularly deep in the admissions office. A point to say, it's not simply "the way the world is" - but something more specific happened in admissions. This is due in large part to the items we have already cataloged, those that correlate with the experience of the 1950s suburban housewives. Those challenges have set the stage for a deeper, more severe, more substantial morale issue than anywhere else on campus.

So, as we review the similarities of experience, let's not lose sight of the fact that for admissions counselors, the items we address in this chapter are additive to what we've already reviewed. There is a cumulative impact that should not be lost if we are to truly understand the problem, and ultimately get to a solution.

The Severity of Severed Human Relationships

Throughout the pandemic, we saw a sudden erosion of our ability to connect with other people. Opportunities to engage directly with peers, supervisors, co-workers across campus, and students were suddenly gone. Both the suddenness and the absence of these connections have caused impacts to the functioning of our society in ways that have not yet been fully understood.

Of course, we tried.

Recognizing that we couldn't meet in person, we all did our best to find virtual substitutes. They were failures, as we now know, but we couldn't have known at the time the sheer magnitude of their failure. To keep the examples simple and accessible to admissions professionals, we need to look no further than learning loss caused by virtual classrooms in high school, middle school, and elementary school.

It has been well documented that the spring semester of 2020 was disrupted, and as such, students shouldn't be held accountable for the disruption. This meant that new freshman students on campus in the fall of 2020 may need to be given a little slack to catch up. This may mean that returning juniors may need a bit more time to go back on the concepts of pre-reqs in courses. Anything less than making those adjustments would be tantamount to punishing students for the crime of having lived through a once-in-a-century global pandemic.

But it wasn't just the spring semester of 2020 that was disrupted. On many, if not most campuses, students were still under restrictions about visitors to their room, social gatherings, masking requirements, etc. Students are reported to have complained to administrators that they felt like "zombies" walking from class to class, without having the full college experience. The entirety of the 2020-2021 academic year experienced some level of disruption that can't be ignored. This was true for students in college, but also true for students in high school, middle school, and earlier.

We now recognize the learning loss from this experience.

It is real.

It is pervasive.

It needs to be addressed.

But who is responsible for the adjustments? If a student lost ground during their freshman year of high school, at what point can they be "caught up" with where they would have been? *Is that even possible?* If so, do they just have their sophomore year to bounce back and be on the same track they would have been without the learning loss, or will they be back on their heels through high school?

Are most colleges prepared to make long-term adjustments, for all students in high school during the pandemic? What about students who were in middle school during the pandemic, and started high school behind? Are we permanently adjusting our definition of college-ready? If we make adjustments to the first-year student experience, must they be "caught up" by the end - or will the impacts of the learning loss stick with them all the way through the achievement of their bachelor's degree? Can we let students earn a bachelor's degree without somehow catching up?

There are profound questions in that stew, and of course neither the challenges nor the solutions are as clear and simple as they might need to be. Students are never "behind" one day and then "caught up" the next. There is never an academic experience where all students finish at the same place. Yet, overall, the power of learning loss from the pandemic is real, and it came from our failed efforts to replicate the in-person learning experience with students for whom that was not an ideal learning environment.

Simply put, the classroom by screen stunted student development. *It also stunted the professional development of employees everywhere - but particularly so on college campuses.*

The campus workplace environment before the pandemic was something special, and difficult to replicate in any other industry. A college vice president once said they love working on campus because, "I get to come to work in a park every day!" - referring to the beautiful campus environment. Others have found a career in higher education to be a ticket to never leaving campus, with the added benefit of not needing to cram for finals. At its most basic, there was a sense of community and attachment to the institution that very rarely exists for folks who work in more corporate or formal institutions.

To fully grasp the specialness of the campus environment, consider the experience of a former Hall Director at a mid-sized regional public institution in Wisconsin. After about 7 years in that role, the time came for him to move on. He was engaged to someone in a major metropolitan area about 45 minutes away from campus, which meant he intended to move to that city. This is a different career path for most hall directors looking to elevate to their next role, as they would normally conduct a national job search, exploring opportunities for advancement anywhere in the country. Like faculty, they "go where the job is" - and figure it out from there. For him, of course, that would not work if he wished to stay near his fiancé, which he very much did.

He would regularly leave his campus to go conduct job interviews in the city. In and around that city are about ten college campuses, public and private, and there was no shortage of job opportunities in higher education. However, he needed to be sure to find a job, so he was also exploring corporate positions. Over lunch in the dining hall, he reflected on the experience.

> "What's interesting is that when I go to a job interview on a college campus, even if I've never been to that college, I know right where I am. I can guess where the dining hall is, where their version of Old Main is, and can start to figure out where the student life office is likely to be. At the same time, when I go to an office building, say the thirteenth floor that is leased by a regional bank and holds 50 cubicles, I feel so out of place."

What this hall director was referencing was the difference in the workplace climate on a college campus versus the corporate world. It has been one of our enduring strengths as employers of choice for mission-driven individuals and those of us who never wanted to leave college.

Of course, that disappeared in an instant for all of us. Whatever sense of community existed from going into the office together vanished for everyone, whether you worked on campus or on the 13th floor of an office building downtown. But the difference between the sense of community we had before and after the pandemic was much more severe for those of us on a college campus. Much like the attempt to replicate human interaction failed for students, so too did the attempt to build working professionals together using tools like Zoom and Teams to replicate the experience of being together.

And no, adding the Zoom feature to all appear on screen like we were in a lecture hall did not help.

They did not replicate the experience.

We were not together anymore.

We've all seen, and tried, all sorts of things during those dark weeks and months as the pandemic was washing over us. Zoom cocktail hours, an open Teams room that anyone could drop in throughout the day, informal Zoom meet ups with no agenda, Teams retirement celebrations.

Every single one of them failed. There was just no replacing the experience of being in personal contact with actual people. Stress, emotional impacts, and mental health challenges came to the forefront in new ways. As a society, we all knew we were "going through something" - but without knowing how long it was going to be or fully understanding how inadequate the replacements would be, we didn't know how deep the rut was, even when we were stuck in it.

Eventually, restrictions faded, or were lifted, and we were able to be together again. If we really had stuck to "two weeks to crush the curve" - it is likely that we all would have come back to the office with a vengeance. Of course, this presumes that the famed curve had been crushed and the risks of disease were lower. It wasn't and we still stayed home for thirty days to crush the curve. Then, throughout the summer, even into the fall, we came back only in rotating waves, never filling our workplaces.

Despite that, we still had goals to meet. While shareholder demands in corporate environments are real, colleges and universities were particularly insatiable in their need for revenue. In either case, the leadership of the organization could not tolerate significant losses of productivity.

This is where the trickery of the American work ethic came into play. Everyone was sent home, and at least for office workers on college campuses, an effort was made to continue to find productive, valuable work that could be done from home. This was an admirable reality of college campuses during this time - we were willing to be incredibly flexible to ensure our staff could continue to work.

Yet, we needed them not just to be employed, we needed them to produce. By produce, we meant that they needed to find ways to be contributing to the unending demands for revenue and enrollment. Whether that was retention efforts, new student enrollment, or pitching the value of living on campus in a very diminished experience, it was all hands on deck.

The folks doing that work, especially when it was outside of their comfort zone, needed to feel valued and appreciated.

So, for weeks, then months, we told everyone working from home how amazing their work was. The flexibility our staff showed, their commitment to finding new ways of working, their ability to remain engaged with students from their kitchen was both impressive and well acknowledged. For a while, it almost seemed to everyone that our work could be done virtually, and the need to be in the office was more perception than necessity.

After all, look how amazing things were when we worked from home.

Something happened along the way. What started as a two-week work from home necessity that everyone would have eagerly shaken off on day 15 started to showcase some new conveniences.

All of us learned that the time we had spent commuting was wasted and we could devote that time to something else. Exercise, for example.

All of us learned that the time we had spent in water cooler conversations between meetings was wasted, and we could use that time for something else. Household chores like laundry or dishes, for example.

All of us learned that the time we had spent in staff meetings did not require our full attention if we could turn our cameras off - and still only ½ of our attention if cameras were on.

In short, all of us learned that there were drawbacks to a centralized, shared workspace that we had never considered.

So, when the time came to call everyone back to campus - there was resistance.

Strong, severe resistance, in some cases.

We had all spent months working from home, proving that we could be just as productive, in ways that were remarkably impressive to college leadership when it was required.

Then, suddenly, we were told that we needed to get back to the commute, the water cooler conversation, the in-person staff meetings for reasons of productivity and community.

This felt like, and was, a complete reversal of the messages being given to employees during the safer at home orders. It is not wrong for our staff members to feel like there was bait and switch. They can be forgiven for coming to conclude that the messages heralding their great work during the pandemic were disingenuous. If college leadership truly believed what they said during the pandemic, there would have been no reason to pull everyone back together.

Of course, there was and is one key reason we need to be together - to restore the loss of human connection. This is not an argument that in person connection is more valuable than the work / life balances we all found during the work-from-home era. But, as has been argued throughout this book, we cannot ignore the negative impacts of our decisions, even if they were correctly decided and necessary. We cannot ignore the negative impacts of the work-from-home era, even as it exists in 2024.

The commute time may appear to have been wasted, but was valuable time to mentally prepare for, or unwind from the workday.

The water cooler conversations did build community, even if there was no clearly measurable impact on the numbers.

And yes, while it may be an unpopular take, coming to a staff meeting with cameras off so you can do something else at the same time does reduce the value of the meeting.

So, when colleges came out of the pandemic and offered partial work-from-home policies, we had the experience of splitting a baby: no one was happy and the baby didn't even make it. When colleges attempted to justify in office requirements by pointing to visitors, admissions counselors would reasonably raise the question about why they were there if the visitors canceled or weren't scheduled for that day. If only half the staff is there on Tuesday, how are we making the argument that this is building community and team cohesion? None of these approaches were successful at replicating the power of the community connection that used to come with the privilege of working full time on a college campus.

Yet, the counter argument was always there. Even if you concede that there's a cumulative value of 200 daily water cooler conversations a year, surely there's nothing wrong with missing just the ones on Monday. A once-a-week work from home policy couldn't be that detrimental to staff cohesion, could it? Perhaps not - but unless the entire office would be closed on Mondays, then staff would need to be rotated. ¼ on Monday, ¼ on Tuesday, etc. So even in that compromise, the positive experience of connection is diminished.

Which leaves the fully returned to normal scenario. In this case, every day that a counselor is forced to commute to campus, or come home to laundry that they couldn't switch in between (or during) meetings, a dishwasher that remains frustratingly filled at the end of the workday becomes a point of frustration, if not anger. Remembering back to how productive they used to be, how celebrated their work from home was, hostility towards their institution was an entirely reasonable reaction.

Yet, like humans generally, they are thinking in the short term, while losing sight of the long-term. They want to give up the work that goes into developing and maintaining connections with their coworkers, perhaps by knowingly pretending that they can be just as effective in that work by Zoom, but they don't want the negative impacts of the lost interpersonal relationships.

This is the experience everyone has been having. For admissions counselors though, it's made even worse because the pandemic, much like erosion at a beach, has revealed just how much their jobs have changed - taking them away from students and turning their faces towards an unending supply of spreadsheets and queries.

The Slow Realization of What Was Lost

A notable effect of the pandemic on all people was the temporary and sudden loss of human connection. While we were no longer together physically, we were also no longer together emotionally. At least in terms of our workplace, we were alone, adrift in an unknown sea with little understanding of how we got there, how long we would be there, and how we would ever get out.

This initiated a society-wide discussion on the importance of human connection. The act of removing us from proximity to each other revealed how important those interactions and engagements actually were. Prior to the pandemic, we spent hours engaging with people and screens combined, to now only be engaging with screens. It was too much - Zoom fatigue was (and remains) real.

What makes the follow-on impacts of the pandemic more difficult for admissions counselors than other groups on campus is that we came to realize a fundamental truth of our profession: we had lost our connection to students. This is the unique, distinguishing effect that is leading admissions counselors to react so differently to their work after the pandemic as compared to other departments.

A question we've all been wrestling with: why are admissions counselors leaving their roles at higher rates than the rest of campus? This is it.

As was outlined earlier, we have slowly evolved the profession *away* from students and *towards* screens. We tried to convince ourselves that these pixels counted as students - but as we learned from Zoom engagement, it's not the same. Queries, spreadsheets, and CRM interfaces are now the biggest group of tasks counselors work on - and every minute of that is time they are not doing work they are passionate about.

Admissions counselors, at least the people we have been hiring to be admissions counselors, feel a drive to help students. That is their infamous "why" - and it is what kept them in positions with salaries that were below what they were worth, with work / life balance expectations in the spring that were beyond manageable, and a travel season that would regularly wear down even the most seasoned admissions professionals. Through all of that, they felt personally rewarded and enriched because of the students they got to work with.

Take the thought experiment from earlier in this book. Imagine going back to the NACAC conference in Milwaukee in 2004, and trying to roll out the sheer volume of spreadsheet work, CRM data entries, and query building they would have to do 20 years in the future. Imagine laying it all out. What parts of the work we have gotten used to would be well-received, and which aspects would they have balked at?

It certainly isn't all bad, but it's also not been a continuous positive march of progress and positivity.

Let's take stock of how the totality of the slow changes in our work are impacting the people that are actually doing the work.

It was certainly true before the modern CRM that counselors were spending a lot of wasted time on targeting the wrong students, right? Therefore, the promise of the CRM to better identify students based on measurable data elements would theoretically be well-received by our peers from a generation ago.

Who could disagree with the assessment that this is a positive development?

Remember that if applications have grown on average 5% a year, there were far fewer applicants back then. Even if application volume remained consistent for counselors (essentially increasing staffing levels by 5% FTE each year) - the average applications per student was much lower. So no, it is not true that a generation ago, the promise of targeting students based on measurable data elements would have been well received - at least not in the intensity of depth it is currently being utilized.

Instead, this benefit to our work became necessary to fix a problem we were in the process of causing for ourselves, with the helpful hand of higher-ed adjacent corporations.

Perhaps the admissions counselors in 2004 would have questioned linking an increase in application rates with a decrease in yield rates and offer a different solution than data targeting an ever-increasing applicant pool.

Sure, but the ability to conduct mass email engagement would create efficiencies, which would have been a needed tool, right? Again, perhaps not.

In 2024, it is not uncommon for admissions counselors to build an email or text message or a campaign for the entire applicant pool, or a subset of it based on one or two key data elements. But twenty years ago, this was not the domain of admissions counselors. If there was a mass message to go out, someone with the developed skill and access to the email program being leveraged by the admissions office would build it - and counselors would work with students individually.

Indeed, the ability for individual counselors to build and deploy mass message email engagement is a feature in the CRM that no one thought to ask for. Now, the ability to manipulate html code, mail merge fields, and the queries behind them are basic skills of admissions counselors.

Certainly, admissions counselors can't remember everything about students, so the "all in one place" aspect of the modern CRM, storing a warehouse of data on individual students would help. Which has some truth, but we have gone to the extreme. What individual things were counselors trying to remember about students twenty years ago?

While it varies by institution, here's a hint: whatever you have elevated to the main page of a student record in your CRM is probably what they needed. Perhaps there are one or two other tabs of application documents that would be there - but that's it.

They certainly did not need *and cannot process* the amount of data we are now collecting on our students. However, the insistence that we all be data-driven (at least in name) creates a drive to use the data since it is there. Knowing the average email engagement rate, although it is important, was not necessary to do our work.

While the modern CRM has made our jobs easier and more efficient, it has also made our jobs less student centric. They have made it easier for us to adopt the moniker of "data-driven" professionals, replacing what we used to be, which is student-driven. Sure, one is not to the exclusion of the other, but as was uncovered in the admissions yield time study, the march towards more and better and deeper uses of data has been slowly creeping into more and more hours of a counselor's job.

Over a generation, we have taken every offering from the modern CRM, and said, 'yes, please!' - without collectively considering how these changes are impacting the experience of our counselors. This is not an indictment of the CRMs or the leaders who eagerly took every new benefit and competitive advantage these systems had to offer. These were the right decisions, but they were incomplete. Every time we added a bit more data work to the average admissions counselor, we didn't ask ourselves what we were taking away.

When the waters of the pandemic receded, it washed away the buildup of changes in our job that we didn't even realize had happened.

It brought into stark relief how much we had drifted away from our core purpose - the experience we were here for.

Admissions counselors do not like where they have drifted.

Today, the job of an admissions counselor, frankly, sucks. While that's a strong statement, what else can explain why admissions counselors are leaving in numbers we've never experienced before *and* in numbers not being experienced in academic affairs, student affairs, or business affairs? Certainly, there are societal changes impacting our counselors, but indeed, there is something unique happening here.

The Admissions Counselor Malaise is here because of the fact that admissions counselors no longer feel the sense of purpose in their work that they once did.

Maybe this chapter has more in common with the experience of 1950s suburban housewives after all.

SO WHAT ARE WE SUPPOSED TO DO?

After taking a "deep dive" into the complex layers of *The Admissions Counselor Malaise*, it becomes clear that while the challenges are daunting, they are not insurmountable. The issues faced by admissions counselors today are the result of a myriad of factors—incremental changes that have compounded over time, altering the very essence of what it meant to be an admissions counselor. But as we look to the future, we find not just challenges but opportunities—opportunities to rethink, reinvigorate, and reshape the profession into one that aligns more closely with its foundational values of student engagement and genuine mentorship.

In this chapter, we transition from diagnosis to action. It's about moving forward with a sense of purpose and a clear vision. The solutions proposed here are not merely patches to cover the symptoms of a deeper issue, but strategic approaches designed to address the root causes of dissatisfaction and disengagement in admissions work. Each solution is a step towards a more fulfilling, sustainable, and effective admissions practice—a practice where the needs of the counselors, the students, and the institution are in harmony.

As we explore these solutions, remember that the goal is not to offer a one-size-fits-all answer but to provide a range of strategies that can be adapted and implemented according to specific institutional needs and cultural contexts. From enhancing onboarding and mentorship programs to reevaluating performance metrics, from harnessing technology to foster efficiency to revitalizing the human connections at the heart of the profession, each solution offers a piece of the puzzle.

Let's embark on this journey with a commitment to change—not just for the sake of our counselors and the students they serve but for the health and future of the educational institutions that rely on the passion and dedication of these essential professionals. This chapter is a call to action, a blueprint for building a more resilient, responsive, and rewarding admissions environment. Let's take these ideas off the page and bring them to life in our workplaces.

Conduct An Honest Assessment

The foundation of any effective solution is a thorough understanding of the problem it seeks to solve. For admissions offices grappling with *The Admissions Counselor Malaise*, the first step must be an honest, comprehensive assessment of counselor dissatisfaction. This involves delving deep into the reasons why admissions counselors may feel disconnected, undervalued, or overwhelmed by their roles.

Admissions leaders need to initiate processes that encourage openness and transparency, which can be facilitated through structured feedback mechanisms such as anonymous surveys, focus groups, and one-on-one interviews conducted by third-party consultants to ensure impartiality. The goal is to create an environment where counselors feel safe to express their true feelings and concerns without fear of repercussion. It is crucial that this assessment goes beyond surface-level inquiries and digs into the nuanced aspects of job dissatisfaction. Leaders should seek to understand not only what aspects of the job are causing stress but also what elements are lacking that could contribute to job satisfaction. Questions could explore areas like workload management, the relevance and effectiveness of training programs, the impact of administrative duties on time available for student interaction, and the adequacy of resources to perform their job effectively.

A major challenge in this process is overcoming inherent biases. Leaders must recognize that their own experiences and successes within the system might blind them to its deficiencies. It's essential to approach this assessment with humility and a willingness to listen and change. This might mean confronting uncomfortable truths about the workplace culture and practices that have been long-standing but are no longer effective or beneficial. Leaders should also be wary of confirmation bias—the tendency to favor information that confirms pre-existing beliefs. When reviewing feedback, it's important to give equal weight to all voices, not just those that echo a leader's own views or the most vocal complaints. Look for patterns and trends in the data, but also pay attention to outlier opinions that might provide unique insights into overlooked issues.

Once the initial assessment is complete, the real work begins. It is not enough to identify the problems; leaders must also commit to acting on the findings. This involves developing a detailed action plan that addresses the specific issues uncovered during the assessment phase. Each action should be paired with measurable outcomes to monitor progress and effectiveness over time. Moreover, this assessment should not be a one-time event. Instead, it should be part of an ongoing dialogue between admissions counselors and leadership. Regular check-ins and follow-up surveys can help institutions adapt to changing circumstances and ensure that the interventions implemented are having the desired effect. Continuous feedback loops will help build trust and show counselors that their input has a direct impact on policy and practice.

Throughout this process, transparency is key. Leaders should communicate openly with their teams about the steps being taken to address dissatisfaction. This includes sharing what changes are being implemented, why they are being made, and how they are expected to improve the working environment. Providing regular updates on the progress of these initiatives can help maintain engagement and buy-in from the team.

Consider the case of a mid-sized university that noticed a high turnover rate among its admissions staff. The leadership conducted an extensive assessment through anonymous surveys and focus groups facilitated by an external party. The findings revealed that while the workload was a significant factor, the lack of professional development opportunities and clarity in career progression also contributed to job dissatisfaction. In response, the university developed a career advancement program specifically for admissions counselors, including clear milestones and skill development opportunities tailored to different career stages. They also implemented a more equitable workload distribution model and increased the number of staff social events to strengthen team bonds. Within a year, employee satisfaction surveys showed a marked improvement, and turnover rates decreased significantly.

Enhance Onboarding and Mentoring Programs

In addressing *The Admissions Counselor Malaise*, it is crucial to reorient the focus towards what originally drew many into the profession: the students. This reorientation involves not just a shift in daily tasks but a cultural shift within the admissions office to prioritize student interactions over mere numerical targets.

The drive to make it "all about the students" must be genuine and visible. Admissions counselors enter the field with a passion for education and a desire to impact young lives positively. Yet, over time, the intensifying focus on metrics like application numbers, yield rates, and net tuition revenue can overshadow the more fulfilling aspects of the job. To counteract this trend, leadership must actively work to ensure that student-centered values are not just stated but are woven into the fabric of daily operations.

Start by celebrating the unique stories and successes of individual students. When a counselor connects a student with the right resources, leading to a breakthrough, or helps a student overcome barriers to submit a successful application, these moments should be highlighted and celebrated. Such recognition reinforces the value of personal touch and directly connects to the counselors' initial motivations.

Furthermore, admissions leaders should consider structuring meetings and communications to regularly include discussions about student success stories, beyond just the numbers. These stories serve as powerful reminders of the impact of their work on individual lives. It shifts the narrative from one of achieving institutional goals to fulfilling the educational aspirations of the students they serve.

Admissions offices might also innovate by creating roles or teams specifically dedicated to student engagement. These roles would focus on building relationships with prospective students through personalized communications and tailored campus experiences, thereby allowing counselors more time to engage deeply with fewer students, rather than superficially managing larger numbers.

Moreover, the use of technology should be evaluated not just for its efficiency but for its ability to enhance meaningful interactions. If a piece of technology or a new system does not serve to deepen the connection between counselors and students, its utility should be questioned. Technology should be a tool for enhancing human interaction, not replacing it.

By realigning the focus of admissions work to be truly student-centered, leaders can cultivate an environment where counselors feel their work is meaningful and impactful. This shift helps to restore the passion and purpose that likely drew them to the field, combating the malaise and fostering a more satisfied and dedicated workforce.

Professional Development and Support

When confronting the long-term impacts of COVID-19, it's crucial for admissions leaders to rethink their strategies and understand that the pandemic has permanently altered the landscape of college admissions and student expectations. COVID-19 isn't just a temporary disruption but a pivotal event that reshaped societal norms, including those surrounding education and work.

During the pandemic, the freeze on student loan payments provided temporary financial relief for millions, which inadvertently shifted public perception and expectations regarding student debt and college affordability. As a result, discussions around debt forgiveness and the true cost of higher education have become more mainstream. Admissions counselors, who are often on the front lines of these discussions with prospective students, have developed a heightened sensitivity to the burden of debt students are asked to bear. This change in perspective is particularly significant among counselors who are recent graduates themselves and may be reevaluating the cost of their own education considering a changed economic landscape.

Institutions need to recognize and address these shifting attitudes in their financial aid policies and recruitment strategies. It's no longer sufficient to assume that traditional models of financial aid and student debt levels are universally acceptable. Admissions leaders must engage in honest dialogues with their teams about the ethics and impacts of financial aid packages. This involves critically assessing whether the financial burden placed on new students aligns with the institution's mission and values, and how these practices affect counselors' perceptions of their roles.

For example, institutions might consider more aggressive financial aid strategies that reduce the need for loans, or even reevaluate the criteria for merit-based versus need-based aid to better align with current economic realities and student needs. By actively involving admissions counselors in these discussions, leaders not only foster a more inclusive decision-making environment but also ensure that policies reflect the concerns and realities of the counselors who interact directly with applicants.

Moreover, the post-pandemic era offers an opportunity to revisit and potentially redesign recruitment and engagement strategies to be more empathetic and responsive to the financial anxieties of prospective students. Admissions offices could develop new communication strategies that more transparently address the realities of student debt and highlight pathways through which the institution supports graduates in achieving financial stability.

This reevaluation isn't just about adapting to the aftermath of the pandemic but is a crucial step in ensuring that higher education remains a transformative experience that is both accessible and equitable. By aligning institutional practices with the evolved expectations of both counselors and students, colleges and universities can rebuild trust and reaffirm their commitment to serving the best interests of their communities.

Become High Tech / High Touch

The challenge of balancing technology with personal interaction is pivotal in reshaping the role of admissions counselors. The modern admissions environment demands a high-tech approach to manage the increasing volumes of applications and data. However, it's equally important to ensure that this technology enhances rather than replaces the personal touch that is crucial in student recruitment.

To address this, admissions offices should aim to create an ecosystem where technology supports and enhances personal interactions rather than overshadowing them. This involves using data analytics and CRM systems to streamline processes and free up counselors to engage more directly with prospective students. For example, data science and machine learning models like we use at enroll ml can help counselors prioritize outreach efforts, focusing their time and energy on students who are most likely to benefit from direct interaction.

Admissions leaders should consider implementing systems that automatically handle routine data tasks, such as initial query sorting or communication tracking. This automation would allow counselors to dedicate more time to one-on-one interactions, personalized follow-ups, and building relationships that are meaningful and impactful.

Furthermore, technology should be leveraged to enhance the counselor's ability to understand and connect with each applicant on a deeper level. Tools that provide insights into a student's interests, concerns, and engagement with the institution can guide counselors on how best to communicate and engage with everyone. By integrating these tools, counselors can offer a more personalized experience that reflects the student's specific needs and aspirations, making the admissions process feel more tailored and considerate.

It is also crucial to provide ongoing training and support for admissions staff to ensure they are not only comfortable but also proficient in using new technologies. This training should not just focus on the operational aspects of the tools but also on how to integrate technology-driven insights into personalized student interactions.

Ultimately, embracing a high tech/high touch approach will not only improve efficiency and effectiveness in recruitment strategies but also enhance the satisfaction and fulfillment of admissions counselors. By ensuring that technology serves to amplify their strengths and capabilities, institutions can create a more dynamic and supportive environment that aligns with the fundamental values of education and mentorship.

Adjust Performance Metrics

It's vital to recognize that the metrics for evaluating admissions directors should differ significantly from those used to assess admissions counselors. The shift in metrics is crucial because the roles they play, while aligned towards the same institutional goals, impact different aspects of the student journey.

Admissions directors often face the pressure of meeting broad institutional targets such as enrollment numbers, application totals, and financial benchmarks. These high-level metrics are essential for strategic planning and long-term institutional health. However, applying the same broad, quantitative-focused metrics to evaluate admissions counselors can obscure the invaluable, mission-driven work they do at a more personal level with prospective students.

Admissions counselors are on the front lines, directly interacting with students. Their success should be measured not just by the volume of applications or enrollments they facilitate, but by the depth and quality of the relationships they build. This relational aspect is critical to both the students' decision-making processes and their initial perceptions of the institution.

To better align performance metrics with the true value admissions counselors bring, institutions should integrate measures that reflect the quality of interactions and the extent to which counselors help prospective students navigate their educational paths. For example, student feedback on campus visit meetings could be a key metric. Such feedback would provide insights into how supported and valued students feel, which is a direct reflection of the counselor's effectiveness in creating a welcoming and informative environment.

Moreover, recognizing counselors for their ability to uphold and transmit the institution's mission should be paramount. Celebrating counselors who go above and beyond to ensure that students understand their potential fit and educational pathways at the institution not only reinforces the importance of mission alignment but also boosts counselor morale and job satisfaction.

Institutions could establish new benchmarks that focus on qualitative achievements, such as the number of meaningful interactions counselors have with prospective students or initiatives counselors undertake to advance equity and access within the admissions process. Recognizing these efforts could include mission-driven awards or acknowledgments during staff meetings, highlighting the role these counselors play in fostering the institutional ethos among the student body.

By shifting the focus from strictly numeric achievements to a balanced evaluation that includes mission-driven activities, institutions can encourage a more holistic approach to admissions. This adjustment ensures that the work of admissions counselors is not just seen as a numbers game but as a crucial part of the educational mission, enhancing both the impact and satisfaction of counselors in their roles.

Recognition and Reward Systems

The nature of the work performed by admissions counselors is unique within the higher education framework, dealing as it does with the pressures of both numbers and deep personal engagement with prospective students. To sustain motivation and recognize the multifaceted nature of their contributions, developing a robust recognition and reward system is critical.

A well-structured recognition system should celebrate achievements that extend beyond traditional metrics like enrollment numbers or application counts. It should highlight efforts that embody the institution's core values, such as inclusivity, personalized student engagement, and innovation in outreach and communication. Recognizing and rewarding these efforts can reinforce a culture of excellence and commitment within the admissions team.

One effective approach could involve implementing periodic awards that acknowledge various aspects of an admissions counselor's work. For example, awards could be given for 'Outstanding Student Advocacy' to honor a counselor who goes above and beyond to assist a student through the application process, or 'Innovative Outreach', recognizing someone who develops new ways to engage potential students that significantly enhance their connection to the institution.

These recognitions should not be limited to formal awards. Informal acknowledgments during team meetings or through internal newsletters can also boost morale and foster a supportive community atmosphere. Public acknowledgment of a counselor's hard work can validate their efforts and help them feel valued by their peers and superiors.

Moreover, rewards should not solely be symbolic. Practical incentives like professional development opportunities, additional vacation days, or flexibility in work schedules can be significant. These benefits not only serve as a reward but also support the personal and professional growth of the counselors, leading to increased job satisfaction and retention.

Institutions should also consider involving admissions counselors in decision-making processes that affect their work. Giving them a voice in shaping the strategies and practices they are expected to implement can serve as both a reward and a motivation, enhancing their commitment to the institution's goals.

By creating a comprehensive recognition and reward system that appreciates both the quantitative and qualitative contributions of admissions counselors, institutions can cultivate an environment where staff feel genuinely appreciated and eager to contribute to their fullest potential. This approach not only enhances the individual counselor's experience but also fundamentally strengthens the institution's ability to attract and retain talented professionals committed to advancing its educational mission.

Work / Life Balance Initiatives

Maintaining a healthy work-life balance is crucial for the wellbeing and effectiveness of admissions counselors, whose roles often involve irregular hours and significant emotional labor. Institutions must implement initiatives that promote a more balanced lifestyle, ensuring that counselors are not only effective in their roles but also content and healthy in their personal lives.

Firstly, institutions can consider flexible working arrangements. Allowing counselors to work remotely or adjust their schedules to accommodate personal commitments can significantly reduce burnout. For instance, during peak recruitment seasons when overtime is common, offering compensatory time off during slower periods can help counselors recharge and maintain their enthusiasm for their work.

Secondly, institutions should invest in resources that support mental health. This could include access to counseling services, workshops on stress management, and training sessions that equip counselors with strategies to handle the emotional aspects of their work. Encouraging a culture where counselors feel comfortable seeking help and discussing their challenges without fear of stigma is vital.

Another impactful initiative could be the creation of peer support groups within the admissions team. These groups can offer a safe space for counselors to share experiences, offer advice, and support each other in balancing the demands of work and personal life. Facilitated by a trained moderator, these groups can help normalize discussions about work-life balance and provide practical solutions tailored to the unique challenges faced by admissions staff.

Moreover, institutions should encourage regular breaks and vacations. Ensuring that counselors actually take time off to disconnect from work responsibilities is essential. Leadership can model this behavior by prioritizing their own work-life balance, demonstrating the institution's commitment to maintaining a healthy working environment.

Lastly, providing professional development opportunities that enhance personal growth can also contribute to a better work-life balance. When counselors feel that their career progression is supported, they are more likely to feel satisfied and balanced in their roles. This could include access to further education, conferences, or skills training that allows them to advance professionally while also enriching their personal development.

By implementing these work-life balance initiatives, institutions not only enhance the productivity and satisfaction of their admissions counselors but also foster a workplace culture that values and supports the wellbeing of its staff. This commitment can lead to higher job satisfaction, lower turnover, and a more motivated and dedicated admissions team.

Community Building Activities

Creating a strong sense of community among admissions counselors is essential for fostering a supportive and collaborative work environment. Community building activities not only enhance the work atmosphere but also provide a network of support that can lead to more effective teamwork and improved job satisfaction.

One effective approach to building community is through regular team-building exercises. These activities can range from simple icebreakers during meetings to organized retreats that allow staff to engage in more extensive, collaborative tasks outside the office environment. Such interactions help break down formal workplace barriers and encourage a more relaxed and open communication among team members.

Moreover, hosting social events can significantly contribute to community building. Whether it's casual lunches, after-work gatherings, or celebratory events marking team achievements, social events provide an informal setting for counselors to bond and build personal connections that strengthen team dynamics. These gatherings need not always be elaborate; even small, spontaneous meetups can be highly effective.

Another key aspect of community building involves professional development workshops that are designed to improve skills while also enhancing teamwork. Workshops can be tailored to address specific areas of interest within the admissions process or broader topics such as leadership development and conflict resolution. When counselors learn together, they grow together, creating a more unified team.

Institutions should also consider creating mentorship programs where more experienced counselors can guide newer staff members. This not only helps in transferring knowledge and refining practices but also establishes a sense of responsibility and belonging among team members. Mentorship fosters an environment where everyone feels valued and supported, enhancing the overall team spirit.

Finally, engaging in community service projects as a team can significantly boost morale and promote a sense of purpose and fulfillment. Participating in charitable activities, whether related to education or broader community needs, allows team members to engage with the community in meaningful ways. This not only strengthens the team but also reinforces the institution's commitment to social responsibility.

By prioritizing these community-building activities, institutions can create a more supportive and cohesive admissions team. This sense of community not only makes the workplace more enjoyable but also enhances collaboration and efficiency, ultimately leading to better outcomes for both the staff and the students they serve.

Strategic Use of Data

In the realm of college admissions, the strategic use of data is paramount not just for achieving institutional goals but also for enhancing the effectiveness and satisfaction of admissions counselors. It's essential to balance the quantitative aspects of data with the qualitative impact it has on counselor operations and student interactions.

Data should be utilized to streamline processes and optimize counselor efforts, focusing on meaningful engagement rather than overwhelming them with excessive metrics. A strategic approach involves identifying key data points that genuinely aid counselors in understanding and responding to prospective students' needs effectively.

One way to achieve this is by implementing predictive analytics that can help counselors prioritize their efforts on students who are most likely to engage and benefit from specific interventions. This doesn't mean bombarding counselors with complex data analysis tasks but rather providing them with actionable insights that are easy to understand and use. For instance, data dashboards can be designed to highlight essential information immediately, such as student interest levels, engagement scores, or likelihood of enrollment. We have seen the transformative power of providing this to counselors in our work at enroll ml.

Furthermore, data should be used to personalize the student experience, which in turn, makes the counselor's job more fulfilling. By leveraging data to tailor communications and interactions, counselors can feel more connected to their work, knowing that they are meeting students' specific needs and interests. This personalized approach not only improves student satisfaction but also enhances the job satisfaction of counselors by providing a clearer sense of purpose and impact.

Institutions should also consider training programs that help counselors effectively use data without becoming overwhelmed. These programs can cover the basics of data interpretation, the use of CRM systems, and how to extract valuable insights without getting bogged down in unnecessary details. The goal is to make data a tool for empowerment, not a source of frustration.

Regular reviews of data practices should be conducted to ensure they remain aligned with the goals of both the institution and the needs of the counselors. This includes assessing the relevance of collected data, the efficiency of data systems, and the overall impact on counselor workload and stress levels. Feedback from counselors should be integral to these reviews, as their firsthand experience will provide critical insights into the practicalities and effectiveness of data strategies.

By strategically using data to enhance rather than complicate the admissions process, institutions can ensure that their counselors are not only more effective in their roles but also more satisfied and engaged with their work. This approach fosters an environment where data serves as a powerful support tool that enhances personal connections and the overall effectiveness of the admissions team.

Let the CRM Data Creep Recede

In the drive to become data-driven, many admissions offices have fallen victim to what can be termed as "CRM data creep"—the gradual and uncontrolled expansion of data collection, analysis, and reporting responsibilities that fall on the shoulders of admissions counselors. This data creep can lead to overwhelming amounts of information, much of which may not be directly actionable or relevant to the counselors' primary tasks of engaging with and recruiting students.

To address this issue, it's crucial for institutions to deliberately scale back the data demands placed on admissions counselors and refocus on the essentials that truly aid in their work. This means prioritizing data that enhances interpersonal connections and decision-making over data that merely fills spreadsheets.

First, admissions leaders should evaluate the data currently required of counselors to determine what is genuinely necessary for effective student engagement and what can be minimized or eliminated. This involves a critical assessment of the metrics that drive admissions strategies—ensuring they are mission-aligned and not just numbers for the sake of numbers. For instance, while it's important to track application numbers and enrollment rates, the minutiae of every interaction or every single email opened by prospective students may not provide meaningful insights and can detract from the primary goal of building relationships.

Second, simplify the interfaces and tools used by counselors. CRM systems should be configured to present only the most pertinent data, customized to the needs of individual counselors based on their specific roles and the strategies of the admissions team. This customization can prevent the feeling of data overload and help counselors focus on their interactions with students rather than navigating through unnecessary information.

Moreover, training for admissions counselors should emphasize efficient data use, teaching them how to quickly extract the insights they need without getting bogged down in complex data

THE ADMISSIONS COUNSELOR MALAISE

analysis. This training should reinforce the idea that CRM tools are there to support their work, not complicate it.

Additionally, consider implementing role-specific data dashboards that automatically highlight the most relevant metrics for each counselor. These dashboards can be designed to focus on relationship-building metrics, such as student engagement levels and interaction histories, rather than overwhelming counselors with every piece of data collected.

Lastly, encourage a culture where feedback on the CRM's effectiveness is regularly solicited and genuinely considered. This feedback loop will help ensure that the CRM evolves in a way that truly supports counselors' work, rather than steering them away from their core mission of student engagement.

By consciously letting the CRM data creep recede, institutions not only enhance the effectiveness of their admissions teams but also protect their counselors from burnout, making the admissions role more sustainable and focused on what truly matters—forming meaningful connections with prospective students.

COMPANION READINGS

The concepts reviewed in this text are in some ways a conglomeration of work and material I've been working on for some time. To that end, I present a collection of items – some podcasts, some blog posts, some research results – all of which roll up to the ideas outlined here.

If the ideas in *The Admissions Counselor Malaise* speak to you and resonate with your experience – perhaps these pieces will as well. If they don't, perhaps you'll find areas of agreement with and disagreement from the conclusions.

In either event, I hope that these additional pieces are additive to your understanding of the staff morale challenges facing our profession – and what the solutions can be.

"Staff Morale Skyrocketed"

May 30, 2023
Webinar hosted by enroll ml
Recording available: crowdcast.io/c/morale/

In my recent webinar, a collaboration with Elizabeth Kirby, Senior Director of Recruitment at Columbia College, we explored pivotal themes around the yield process time study—specifically, its implications on staff morale within the admissions offices of higher education institutions. This webinar is part of a larger discourse that I've addressed in this book focusing on the emerging crisis of staff morale in college admissions. Given the strategic importance of this topic, the insights shared during the webinar are crucial for both understanding and addressing the ongoing challenges that our admissions teams face daily.

Our discussion was not just about numbers and conversion rates; it delved deeper into the human elements that drive the admissions process—elements that are often overshadowed by the pressing need to meet enrollment targets. The yield process time study, conducted by our team at Enroll ML, served as a foundational piece of research, revealing not only inefficiencies in traditional recruitment methods but also the significant impact these practices have on the morale and well-being of staff.

Elizabeth's insights, paired with my own experiences, underscored a critical narrative: the need to shift our focus from merely enhancing procedural efficiencies to nurturing the emotional and professional well-being of our teams. This webinar serves as a bridge between the theoretical frameworks discussed in my book and the practical, real-world application of these ideas.

As we move forward in this summary, we will delve into the specific takeaways from our study, focusing particularly on the challenges and solutions related to staff morale. I encourage you to view this webinar to fully grasp the depth of our discussion and to see these strategies in action.

One of the central themes we explored during our webinar was the concept of "the three," a perspective popular at Enroll ML to evaluate the opportunities to get three more applicants to enroll, out of every 100. This strategy emphasizes a nuanced approach to the admissions process, shifting focus from sheer numbers to understanding the reasons behind each student's decision. The goal is to identify opportunities where we could potentially convert a 'maybe' into a 'yes,' thus enhancing our overall yield without significantly increasing the number of applications.

This approach does more than just improve yield rates; it also has profound implications for how we manage and support our admissions staff. By focusing on quality interactions and deeper engagement with fewer candidates, our team can operate in a less frantic, more focused environment. This shift can significantly alleviate the stress and burnout commonly experienced in admissions roles, which are often exacerbated by high-volume, high-pressure recruitment tactics.

The importance of understanding these enrollment dynamics cannot be overstated. It forms the crux of how we can better support our staff by providing them with tools and strategies that not only make their work more effective but also more fulfilling. As we delve into the specifics of staff morale issues in the next section, it's essential to keep in mind that our approach to enrollment fundamentally shapes the workplace culture and the well-being of our admissions counselors.

By adopting strategies like "the three," we begin to see a shift in how admissions teams perceive and engage with their work, laying a foundation for addressing the broader morale challenges that will be discussed in the following sections. This is where our theoretical discussions intersect with practical applications, revealing the potential for significant positive change in both staff satisfaction and student enrollment outcomes.

During the webinar, a significant focus was placed on the morale issues uncovered by our yield process time study. The findings highlighted a critical, often overlooked aspect of admissions work: the well-being of our staff. Over the last two decades, the role of admissions counselors has subtly yet profoundly shifted, inadvertently increasing their stress levels and impacting their job satisfaction. This evolution has moved away from relationship-building and mentoring potential students towards a more transactional model driven by numbers and immediate results.

The implications of these changes are far-reaching. Admissions counselors, once motivated by the opportunity to guide prospective students through one of their most important life decisions, now find themselves mired in a cycle of enrollment goals and performance metrics. This shift not only diminishes their job satisfaction but also their effectiveness, as a disengaged counselor is less likely to foster the connections necessary for a prospective student to commit to an institution.

Our discussion underscored the necessity of reevaluating how these roles are structured and supported. By acknowledging and addressing the sources of stress and dissatisfaction among staff, institutions can begin to rebuild a culture that values and supports the well-being of every team member. Solutions such as providing better resources for dealing with emotional fatigue, restructuring targets to be more realistic and humane, and fostering a workplace environment that promotes balance and wellness are vital.

It's clear that addressing these challenges is not just a matter of operational efficiency but also of ethical leadership and organizational health. The strategies we explored, particularly focusing on the well-being of admissions staff, are integral to creating a supportive environment that enhances both employee satisfaction and student enrollment outcomes.

The insights from our webinar underscore the importance of rethinking traditional recruitment tactics and focusing more on the human elements that drive successful enrollments. By adopting more humane and strategic approaches to admissions, we can ensure that our institutions not only thrive in terms of numbers but also in terms of the quality and engagement of the staff who drive these numbers.

I encourage all readers to view the full webinar to engage deeply with the detailed discussions and solutions provided. There, you'll gain a richer understanding of how these strategies can be implemented in your own institutions. This webinar is not just a resource but a call to action for all higher education leaders to prioritize the well-being of their teams as a fundamental component of their enrollment strategies.

By fostering a culture that values and supports admissions counselors, we pave the way for a more resilient and effective admissions process that can meet the challenges of today and tomorrow. Let's commit to these changes and watch as our institutions, staff, and students flourish together.

Counselor Retention

November 1, 2022
The Admissions Directors Lunchcast Podcast
Streaming: https://podcasters.spotify.com/pod/show/adlunchcast/

In The Admissions Counselor Malaise, we delve deeply into the challenges admissions counselors face today. A particularly pressing issue is counselor retention during the Great Resignation. In episode #31 of the Admissions Directors Lunch Cast, which I co-host with Nathan Ament, we engage with two seasoned professionals who provide invaluable perspectives on this matter.

The episode features Amanda Booth, Director of College Counseling at Wichita Collegiate School, and Julie Nelson, Assistant Dean of Admissions at Xavier University. Their insights highlight the critical need for stability and consistency in admissions teams—factors that are crucial for building and maintaining effective relationships with high schools and ensuring trust in the admissions process.

Amanda Booth stresses the importance of consistent counselor presence, which fosters reliable relationships crucial for effective student recruitment. Her dual experience on both the high school and college sides of admissions provides a unique vantage point on how high turnover rates hinder relationship-building efforts and disrupt trust.

Julie Nelson discusses how the role of admissions counselors has evolved to require a broad skill set that includes not only student recruitment but also data analysis, digital marketing, and extensive personal interaction with prospective students. She emphasizes that the demanding nature of these roles, coupled with insufficient compensation and professional development, leads to burnout and high turnover rates.

Both guests underscore the necessity of reevaluating support structures and career progression opportunities for admissions counselors. They advocate for creating a supportive work environment where counselors feel valued beyond their immediate recruitment results and have access to opportunities for professional growth.

As hosts, Nathan and I reflect on the importance of these strategies in retaining talented staff and maintaining the quality of engagement with prospective students and their advisors. Listening to the experiences and advice shared by Booth and Nelson can provide admissions directors and their teams with actionable insights into fostering more resilient and effective admissions offices.

For those grappling with counselor retention issues, I highly recommend listening to this episode. It serves as a vital resource, offering context and concrete examples of how strategic engagement and thoughtful management practices can significantly mitigate the impacts of the Great Resignation within our institutions.

This episode not only complements the themes discussed in The Admissions Counselor Malaise but also provides essential insights into improving the stability and efficacy of our admissions teams in these challenging times.

Modernizing Enrollment Management

January 26, 2024
Higher Ed Marketing Lab Podcast, by Echo Delta
Streaming: https://open.spotify.com/show/69JSoHsVGxsAoj5RCf6NUi

As we peel back the layers of challenges faced by admissions counselors outlined in The Admissions Counselor Malaise, it becomes clear that traditional approaches often fall short in addressing the complexities of today's educational landscape. In the quest for solutions, it's essential to look beyond the confines of traditional higher education paradigms. Enter Geoff Baird, a figure whose background in business, finance, and technology offers a fresh and necessary perspective. His recent podcast episode on modernizing enrollment management not only complements the discussions in this book but also extends a bridge towards actionable change.

Geoff's approach, rooted in a deep understanding of market dynamics and technological innovation, challenges the status quo of higher education administration. His insights underscore the necessity of adopting a mindset that views students not just as learners but as consumers. This shift is crucial for institutions aiming to thrive in an increasingly competitive environment. By leveraging techniques from the business world, schools can enhance their operational efficiency and more effectively meet the needs of their students and staff.

The podcast dives deep into the practical application of these ideas, particularly through the use of advanced technology to streamline and enhance enrollment strategies. Geoff discusses how machine learning and data analytics can transform the recruitment process by enabling more personalized and effective engagement with prospective students. He emphasizes the importance of understanding the student's journey from initial contact through to enrollment, suggesting that a more granular approach to data can significantly improve yield rates.

For admissions counselors, who are often on the front lines of these challenges, Geoff's strategies offer a new glimmer of hope.

Implementing technology to handle routine tasks can free up time for more meaningful interactions with students, ultimately leading to higher job satisfaction and reduced burnout. Moreover, by redefining performance metrics to focus on mission-driven outcomes rather than just numbers, counselors can feel more connected to their work and its impact.

To truly grasp the depth and applicability of Geoff's insights, I encourage all readers of this book to listen to his podcast. It's not only an extension of the conversation on how to combat the malaise affecting admissions counselors but also a guide on implementing these modern strategies effectively. The episode is available on the Higher Ed Marketing Lab website, and it promises to be a thought-provoking exploration of how business acumen can intersect with educational goals to foster a more dynamic and responsive admissions environment.

Let's remember that the journey towards revitalizing our admissions offices is ongoing. Openness to external perspectives like Geoff's not only enriches our strategies but also ensures we remain adaptable in a rapidly changing world. Engage with the podcast, reflect on its lessons, and consider how you might apply these modern approaches within your own institutions. Together, we can redefine the future of enrollment management, making it more efficient, more effective, and more aligned with the evolving needs of our students and staff.

TEEGE METTILLE

Staff Development During The Great Resignation

March 14, 2023
The Admissions Directors Lunchcast Podcast
Streaming: https://podcasters.spotify.com/pod/show/adlunchcast/

In addressing the challenges highlighted in The Admissions Counselor Malaise, it is critical now more than ever to focus on the morale of admissions counselors. An excellent resource that offers valuable insights and practical strategies for achieving this is episode #34 of the "Admissions Directors Lunch Cast." Co-hosted by me and Nathan Ament, this episode delves into staff development during the Great Resignation, a period marked by high turnover and changing job expectations within the admissions profession.

The podcast features enlightening contributions from Marion Meadows, at the time, the president-elect of Ohio ACAC, and director of county programs at "I Know I Can" in Columbus, Ohio. Marion emphasizes the importance of building personal connections with students to enhance counselor impact and satisfaction. Her approach suggests that direct communication, rather than relying solely on emails, can foster meaningful relationships that not only benefit student recruitment but also enhance counselor engagement and job satisfaction.

Seinquis Leinen, at the time, the president of Dakota ACAC and director of admission at North Dakota State University, offers another perspective on handling staff turnover. She shares innovative practices implemented at her institution to maintain staff morale. Seinquis highlights the adoption of flexible work policies and the importance of continuous staff development as key strategies. By providing opportunities for growth and adapting to the needs of the team, North Dakota State University has created a supportive environment that motivates staff and reduces the likelihood of turnover.

Both Marion and Seinquis provide actionable advice for admissions directors facing similar challenges. For instance, Marion's focus on personal outreach demonstrates how counselors can effectively

142

engage students in a manner that feels individualized and caring. Seinquis's approach to flexible work arrangements and her proactive stance on staff development illustrate how institutions can adapt to modern workplace demands, thereby retaining talented staff.

I encourage readers of The Admissions Counselor Malaise to listen to this podcast episode. The insights from Marion Meadows and Seinquis Leinen are particularly relevant as they echo the need for renewed focus on counselor morale—a crucial theme in our ongoing discussion about improving the admissions environment. By integrating some of the strategies discussed in the podcast, admissions leaders can take meaningful steps towards addressing the counselor malaise that has become all too common in our field.

This episode serves as a potent companion piece to our exploration in The Admissions Counselor Malaise, offering not just corroborative insights but also tangible, actionable strategies that can help revitalize the morale of admissions teams across the country.

The Admissions Time Study

Over the course of 2023, I led a comprehensive research project known as the Admissions Time Study. The results were presented as webinars exclusive for MACRAO (Montana) and NJACAC. This endeavor aimed to dissect and refine the yield processes in college admissions using data-driven analysis. The profound insights we uncovered highlight actionable strategies that admissions officers can implement to optimize their recruitment efforts.

Purpose of the Study

The primary goal of this time study was to critically evaluate the existing admissions processes to identify inefficiencies and areas for improvement. At enroll ml, we harness the power of artificial intelligence and data science to enhance yield recovery from admissions activities, helping colleges tap into a pool of potential students who might otherwise be overlooked. Through this research, we sought to understand the daily realities of admissions counselors, the challenges they face, and how technology might both hinder and help in achieving their enrollment goals.

Methodology

To conduct this study, we employed a qualitative approach that involved in-depth interviews with admissions leaders from a variety of institutions. We focused on analyzing 44 distinct tasks integral to the admissions cycle, aiming to capture a holistic view of where time and resources were being spent. Our participants included leaders responsible for supervising a collective total of 217 counselors, each bringing an average of 19 years of experience. These leaders managed teams averaging ten counselors, providing a broad perspective on the admissions landscape.

Key Findings

One of the most significant findings was the evolving role of admissions counselors over the past twenty years, coinciding with the rise of modern CRM systems. Traditionally tasked with engaging directly with prospective students, counselors now spend a considerable amount of time navigating data-driven tasks. Our study highlighted that admissions counselors spend about 657 hours per year on data mining activities within CRMs, which significantly detracts from their time spent in direct interaction with students. This shift underscores a move towards administrative tasks, which may impact the effectiveness of personal recruitment efforts.

Core Thesis of the Study

Our research led to the development of three main theses regarding the state of college admissions:

The Accidental Shift: The introduction and capabilities of modern CRMs have inadvertently shifted the focus of admissions counselors from student interaction to data management. This shift has led to an increase in administrative tasks, reducing the time available for engaging directly with prospective students.

The Myth of Magic Leads: There is no secret stash of leads or a magical solution that will instantly boost enrollment numbers. Sustainable increases in enrollment result from strategic, ongoing recruitment efforts rather than quick fixes or miraculous discoveries.

Resource Constraints: The resources traditionally relied upon to boost enrollment, such as financial discounting and the energy and morale of admissions teams, are increasingly strained. These limitations highlight the need for innovative approaches to meet growing enrollment targets without overextending current capabilities.

Strategic Recommendations for Admissions Officers

Based on our comprehensive analysis, we recommend several strategies for admissions officers to enhance their recruitment processes:

Focus on High-Probability Enrollees: Develop a system to identify and monitor students who show a high likelihood of enrollment based on predictive analytics. Engage these students judiciously to ensure efficient use of resources.

Streamline Efforts for Low-Probability Enrollees: Implement measures to reduce intensive outreach to students who demonstrate minimal engagement or interest. By reallocating these resources, admissions teams can focus more effectively on more promising prospects.

Prioritize Engagement with Swing Students: Dedicate additional resources to students who are undecided but show potential for conversion. This group requires the most personalized attention and detailed follow-up but also presents the greatest opportunity for positively influencing yield rates.

Impact and Future Implications

The findings from the Admissions Time Study are critical for rethinking how admissions offices use technology and allocate their human resources. By shifting back towards more personal interactions and reducing the emphasis on data-heavy tasks, institutions can not only improve their yield outcomes but also enhance job satisfaction among their admissions staff.

Call to Action

The enroll ml Time Study has shed light on the essential changes needed within the admissions process and offered practical strategies for improvement. For those interested in delving deeper into our findings and exploring the detailed discussions from the study, I highly recommend watching the full webinar. The recording can be accessed via the link provided at the top of this section, serving as a valuable resource for anyone aiming to refine their admissions strategies and achieve superior results in today's competitive educational environment.

They Prefer Comfortable Conversations

October 5, 2022
Blog post
Archived at: https://www.enrollml.com/post/they-prefer-comfortable-conversations

Your admissions counselor wants to feel good about the work they do and that they are contributing to the ultimate goal.

Ironically, it is this drive that is preventing you from increasing yield.

When you have a conversation with a student who is skeptical about enrolling at your institution, is actively considering an alternative, and is asking many probing questions, you feel like there is a good chance the student doesn't enroll.

When you have a conversation with a student who is all but decided about enrolling at your institution, views your institution as better than the alternative, and is mainly asking questions to reinforce your strengths, you leave feeling like there is a good chance the student does enroll.

So, naturally, admissions counselors are drawn toward the second conversation. They're comfortable, they're easy, and they feel good.

However, it was the first type of conversation – the awkward, uncomfortable, challenging conversation that is actually improving your yield. The student asking difficult, probing questions isn't doing it to prove a point or to make you feel bad – they are doing it because they genuinely want the answers and to feel good about enrolling at your institution.

If your counselor doesn't have the awkward conversation with them, one of two things will happen:

The other college they are considering will and have a better chance of enrolling that student

The other college also shies away from the awkward conversation, and both institutions are leaving it up to chance to see where the student lands

Of course, your counselor doesn't know what type of student is waiting for them after their campus tour. I'm not suggesting that counselors are bobbing and weaving out of these conversations – but their training, impulses, and personal biases guide them towards scheduling and engaging in more comfortable conversations than uncomfortable ones.

Think about it. Who is more likely to schedule the visit to even have the individual post-tour meeting? Who is more likely to answer the phone when they see your institution is calling? Who is more likely to reply to an email asking a question? Who is more likely to participate in a zoom event?

Comfortable, comfortable, comfortable, and comfortable.

At every turn, the infrastructure for how we do our work draws out comfortable conversations.

To improve the yield potential within your recruitment strategy, your counselors need to dig deeper into their applicant pool, be more intrusive with scheduling requests and initiating conversations, and look for opportunities to answer difficult questions from students.

The outcome range of your strategy is shrinking every day. Having a comfortable conversation with an already persuaded student has minimal impact. But each day, you miss an opportunity to hang on to a student who has yet to be persuaded is time lost that cannot be recovered.

Your Counselors Are Unhappy ... Do Something About It

November 2, 2022
Blog post
Archived at: https://www.enrollml.com/post/your-counselors-are-unhappy-do-something-about-it

There are actions admissions directors can take today to improve job satisfaction on their team.

Admissions Directors cannot solve most problems leading to unhappy admissions counselors. But you are not powerless. You can and should do things right now to improve your team's work environment.

It will be no surprise to anyone reading this that there is a staffing crisis in admissions. At every level, from new counselors to experienced vice presidents, there has been an exodus out of admissions and off college campuses.

I myself am one of the recent campus exiles – so the discussions at the NACAC conference were of particular interest. There were several sessions about The Great Resignation, the buzz throughout the exhibit hall was about offsetting staffing challenges, and perhaps the most telling indicator – the longest line was not at Starbucks; it was at the free headshot booth.

Indeed, The Great Resignation has hit us hard and it is showing no signs of slowing down.

While I am not professing to know all the reasons or offer all the solutions, there are a few elements within the control of admissions directors.

Here are a few things to consider. In the coming weeks, I'll make sure to unpack each point with some ideas on what you can do today to reduce the likelihood of one of your counselors resigning tomorrow.

Why are counselors unhappy in their work? Hare are three reasons that you do have direct control over:

They're told to build relationships with families, but 'having great conversations' with students already likely to enroll does not equal hitting enrollment goals. When they feel good about the students they talk to but the numbers don't come in, they can feel defeated, and, worse, misled.

Admissions directors are usually unable to clearly and plainly show which students in an admit pool need a personal, time-intensive intervention from their counselor. In the absence of that, we are giving them call lists that are way too long, or worse, not asking them to call because the long lists were dispiriting.

The internal motivations of an admissions counselor do not neatly align with the most effective recruitment strategies. When left to prioritize their outreach (so as not to leave them feeling micromanaged), they end up spinning their wheels on comfortable, efficient communication methods that are not effective.

As an admissions director, you may be unable to change salary levels, although you should try.

You cannot set the terms of the on-campus / work-from-home expectations of University leadership.

It is not in your power to make the student decision process easy and comfortable for admissions counselors.

But you can and should take action to improve the three pain points above that your admissions counselors are struggling with.

Our Jobs Weren't Designed This Way

May 18, 2023
Blog post
Archived at: https://www.enrollml.com/post/our-jobs-werent-designed-this-way

What on earth were we thinking?

That's a genuine question I have for my friends and colleagues, those of us who have been admissions leaders over the last generation. What were we thinking when we created this work environment for admissions counselors?

Staff morale in admissions offices is as bad as it has ever been. At first, we could maybe convince ourselves that it was just The Great Resignation hitting us like everyone else. But that's not true – it's much worse here.

Here's why: over the course of a generation, we have slowly changed the job of admissions counselors, and right now, quite frankly, it sucks.

In order to achieve short-term objectives, we have bloated the applicant pool of each of our admissions counselors to the point that no individual person can be expected to manage them in a personal, relational way. Just to add insult to injury, every time we made this problem worse, we sent out a celebratory press release!

With this ever-expanding applicant pool, we are still holding on to the level of personal outreach and engagement with students that we were trained on when we started. But with a 5% increase in the applicant pool every year, surely we can't keep increasing our contacts by 5% – there is a human limit. That's something we somehow left out of our press releases.

So this problem we've created by bloating our applicant pool has created a need for a new skill set among admissions counselors – data analysis and mining. If we still need to be as personal and relational in our recruiting, but the applicant pool has grown by 50-75% in the last fifteen years, then we have no choice but to identify which students will get that engagement. Failing to do this means we're equally spreading our most precious resource, time, across the entire applicant pool, diluting the effect.

Now, we have a core skill: data analysis, which is at odds with what we hire people to do. When hiring admissions counselors, we usually look for energetic, outgoing, effervescent people who get excited about the prospect of talking to prospective students about their future and how this institution could be a good fit for them.

That's why most admissions counselors are accepting jobs in our profession.

But they get here, and then we sit them at a desk and put them behind a screen reviewing data records for, on average, 2 ½ hours per day. That's looking through spreadsheets, queries, contact reports, CRM records; you name it. That's before a single conversation with a student – it's all just data analysis.

To be clear – that figure comes from quantitative research I have been conducting with admissions leaders. Currently covering over 200 admissions counselors, the average time reported on reviewing data for student contacts is, on average, 627 hours per year, or 2 ½ hours per day.

None of us meant for this to happen, but we all played a part in creating it. So now we must change it – we have to change the job of an admissions counselor back to what it was – working closely with individual students.

Counselors Are Chasing the Wrong Students

May 25, 2023
Blog post
Archived at: www.enrollml.com/post/counselors-are-chasing-the-wrong-students

Whatever day you're reading this, if you're an admissions director, ask yourself this question: which students are your counselors reaching out to today?

Who did they reach out to on February 17? What about October 9?

Were they the right students?

I raise this question because I think counselors are chasing the wrong people on balance. Not intentionally – it appears that in most cases, neither the admissions counselor nor the admissions leader can accurately identify the right students to reach out to. So, they cast a wide net and let loose their most precious resource, an admissions counselor's time.

Imagine being able to break out your admit pool by demonstrated interest with the level of accuracy on this chart. In each of the buckets, students are scored by the behaviors they've shown indicating interest in enrolling, and each bucket has a corollary probability of enrollment that is validated by the highest levels of data science and machine learning.

If you had access to this information, how would you answer the question of, "Who are your counselors reaching out to today?"

Without access to this chart, perhaps you'd tell a counselor to contact a certain number of students this week. Which students will they be drawn to? If they're like most of us, they'll be drawn to students at the top of the chart with the highest probability of enrollment. Those students are already hooked; the conversations are fun, engaging, and affirming. But when they spend time re-engaging with students who are already at a 90% probability of enrolling, they're not helping to improve enrollment.

Without access to this chart, perhaps you'd generate a call list from their applicant pool, maybe limiting it based on the FAFSA or visits. But you'll also certainly catch a huge chunk of students at the bottom, with virtually no probability of enrollment. This will lead to short, abrupt, or even rude conversations, hang-ups, etc. This is demoralizing to your counselors.

With access to this chart, however, you can correctly identify the students who are interested, engaged, and considering your institution but not yet sold. This is where the conversations are the toughest, as students will ask probing questions, but they are also the most productive. Here, you can identify your swing students – the students who will make or break your class this year.

This chart is just one way to do it, but admissions directors everywhere need to have a very specific, data-sound way of identifying their swing students. If not, chances are good that your counselors spend much of their time chasing the wrong students.

Which means you and your counselors are missing opportunities.

Boosting Counselor Morale

November 29, 2023
Blog post
Archived at: https://www.enrollml.com/post/boosting-counselor-morale-a-critical-element-for-enrollment-success

Enrollment success is the collective achievement of an institution, and the morale of your admissions counselors plays a vital role in this success.

Counselor Morale: A Hidden Catalyst for Success

Admissions counselors are at the forefront of your institution's student recruitment efforts. They are the bridge between your institution and prospective students, providing guidance, answering questions, and fostering connections. Their morale directly influences the quality of these interactions and, subsequently, the enrollment numbers.

High morale among counselors leads to increased motivation, job satisfaction, and a more positive outlook on their responsibilities and the institution. It results in a more enthusiastic and effective team that approaches their tasks with self-renewing vigor. When counselors feel valued and supported, they are better equipped to engage with students and effectively convey the unique qualities of your institution.

On the other hand, low morale can lead to burnout, decreased performance, and attrition. Counselors who feel overwhelmed, undervalued, or disconnected from the institution's mission are less likely to provide the level of commitment and personalized support that prospective students need.

The Role of Data-Science-Driven Insights

enroll ml recognizes that boosting counselor morale is a multifaceted task that requires a strategic approach. Ordering pizza during a calling night isn't going to cut it.

Data-science-driven insights can provide valuable information about counselor performance, workloads, and student interactions. These insights enable admissions leaders to identify areas for improvement, recognize exceptional efforts, and offer targeted support.

With data science at your disposal, you can make informed decisions to create a supportive and empowering work environment for your admissions counselors. This can involve adjustments to workload, recognition of achievements, and personalized professional development opportunities. When counselors feel that their contributions are recognized and supported, their morale improves, which directly benefits enrollment success.

Strategies to Boost Counselor Morale

Boosting counselor morale isn't just about recognizing the importance of their role; it's also about implementing strategies that lead to real change. Here are some approaches to consider:

1. Recognition and Reward

Implement a system for recognizing and rewarding exceptional counselor performance. This can be linked to specific enrollment goals or exceptional interactions with students. Look for opportunities small and large – a concept that enroll ml users recognize in the "Counselor High Fives" section of the app.

2. Professional Development

Provide opportunities for ongoing professional development and skill enhancement. When counselors feel that they are growing in their role, their morale improves.

3. Data-Science-Driven Targeting

Lean on emerging data science technology like enroll ml to pinpoint students who need personalized support, directing counselors' efforts to the most important and most rewarding conversations with prospective students.

4. Transparent Communication

Ensure open and transparent communication between counselors and leaders. Encourage feedback loops and involve counselors in decisions that affect their work.

5. Feedback Loop

Implement a feedback loop using data science insights to inform counselors about their impact on students, helping them adjust their strategies to create more meaningful interactions.

Counselor Morale Matters

In the competitive landscape of higher education admissions, the morale of your admissions counselors is a hidden catalyst for enrollment success. By recognizing the significance of their role, using data-driven insights, and implementing morale-boosting strategies, your institution can foster a motivated and effective team. The result is a more engaging and student-centric admissions approach, which directly impacts enrollment outcomes.

NACAC Conference Bonus: Morale and Burnout

September 23, 2023
The Admissions Directors Lunchcast Podcast
Streaming: https://podcasters.spotify.com/pod/show/adlunchcast/

In a recent episode of our podcast, Nathan and I addressed the pressing issue of burnout and morale among admissions professionals, sparked by a comprehensive survey involving hundreds of professionals across the field. The survey illuminated significant challenges and underscored the critical need for effective leadership in mitigating these issues. This discussion is particularly enriched by the contributions of Seinquis Leinen and Jessica Sant, seasoned experts whose insights significantly influence the discourse on leadership and its impact on workplace wellness.

Leadership fundamentally shapes the workplace environment and is pivotal in either exacerbating or alleviating staff burnout. Jessica Sant, the Chief Engagement Officer at the Lovett School in Atlanta, GA, emphasizes that leaders set the tone for the organizational culture. Effective leadership goes beyond mere management to actively cultivating a work environment that promotes well-being and sustainability. Leaders who prioritize clear communication, realistic goal setting, and acknowledge the personal boundaries of their team can drastically reduce feelings of burnout. Such leaders not only advocate for healthy work practices but also demonstrate them, setting a powerful example for their teams.

One of the crucial roles of leaders in educational settings, as discussed by Sant, is to model the behaviors they wish to see in their colleagues. For instance, by not sending emails during weekends or late at night, leaders can signal the importance of work-life balance to their teams. This practice helps in setting healthy boundaries that discourage round-the-clock work expectations, thus preventing burnout. Sant suggests that effective leadership involves visible actions that reflect a commitment to the well-being of the staff, which in turn fosters a supportive and productive work environment.

Seinquis Leinen, Director of Admission at North Dakota State University, shares insights from her own leadership journey, highlighting the transition from high-availability expectations to advocating for well-being and self-care among her team. She discusses the importance of leaders being self-aware and taking care of their own needs as a means to better support their teams. Empowering leadership involves trusting team members, delegating effectively, and recognizing the diverse needs of individual team members, thereby fostering a culture where staff feel valued and supported.

Both Seinquis and Jessica underscore the significant importance of professional development and community building as essential tools in combating burnout. They advocate for creating opportunities for staff to connect, share experiences, and grow together, which enhances morale and reduces the isolation that often accompanies burnout. The podcast discusses how fostering a sense of community among educational professionals—through conferences, workshops, and informal gatherings—can provide the support and motivation needed to navigate the challenges of the admissions field.

The insights from Jessica and Seinquis illuminate the crucial role of leadership in addressing burnout and morale issues within the educational sector. Their experiences and strategies provide a roadmap for leaders looking to cultivate a healthier work environment. As we continue to navigate the complexities of education and admissions, it becomes increasingly clear that proactive and empathetic leadership is not just beneficial but essential. For a deeper exploration of these themes and practical advice from seasoned professionals, we encourage listeners to access the full podcast episode, available at the link provided in the book. This resource is invaluable for anyone looking to enhance their leadership skills and foster a more supportive workplace.

Oatmeal Insights

Teege Mettille
Unpublished Blog Post
Not Available Online

In a world increasingly dominated by the relentless pursuit of profit, the pervasive influence of corporations has transcended the boundaries of commerce and industry, infiltrating the very sanctuaries of learning and personal development—our colleges and universities. This profound shift in focus, from the holistic nurturing of minds to the relentless maximization of financial gain, poses not just a dilemma but a dire threat to the foundational principles upon which the academic world was built.

The book Corporation Nation by Charles Derber, initially published at the dawn of the new millennium, was prophetic in its dissection of this creeping corporate ethos. Derber, a seasoned observer of societal patterns and a Sociology Professor at Boston College, delved into the mechanics of corporate dominance with a clarity that was both incisive and unsettling. He presented a scenario where corporations, these behemoths of power, have not merely expanded their reach but have reshaped every aspect of life in their image.

Leveraging insights from Betty Friedan's seminal work, The Feminine Mystique, Derber explored how economic uncertainties of the 1990s catalyzed a transformation in American identity— where the values of community and collaboration were overshadowed by a stark individualism fueled by corporate interests. This transformation, while dissected within the context of corporate influence on individual lives, mirrors the alarming evolution we witness today in institutions of higher learning.

These institutions, once revered as epicenters of knowledge and cultural development, are increasingly mirroring the corporate model—prioritizing revenue generation over the sanctity of education. This fundamental realignment, subtly yet steadily, has redrawn the very purpose of education from one of intellectual and moral development to a stark equation of profit and loss.

How did we come to this point? What forces propelled our esteemed academic institutions to adopt a blueprint that seems so starkly at odds with their noble missions? The answers to these questions lie not only in the financial statements of universities but in the very fabric of our societal values, which have increasingly come to celebrate financial gain as the ultimate measure of success.

At the heart of this discussion stands a poignant observation made by Kenneth Mason, the then-President of Quaker Oats, who articulated a truth so fundamental yet so frequently overlooked: "Making a profit is no more the purpose of a corporation than getting enough to eat is the purpose of life. Getting enough to eat is a requirement of life; life's purpose, one would hope, is somewhat broader and more challenging. Likewise with business and profit."

This statement, steeped in wisdom, serves as a clarion call for a reevaluation of our priorities. Mason's analogy between the basic human necessity of sustenance and the corporate drive for profit draws a stark parallel to the current state of higher education. Just as sustenance supports the body but does not define the richness of life, net tuition revenue, while necessary for operational stability, should not overshadow the deeper mission of educational institutions.

Yet, in an age where fiscal pressures loom large, this fundamental truth seems to have been relegated to the footnotes of university agendas. The transformation is evident: colleges and universities, once bastions of learning and character-building, now operate under models strikingly similar to those of corporations, where the drive for financial gain often trumps the educational and developmental needs of the students they vow to serve.

Mason's perspective is both a warning and a guidepost. It prompts us to question: If the purpose of education is broadened to encompass more than the transmission of knowledge—if it is indeed about shaping well-rounded, critically thinking individuals— then how can institutions justify a primary focus on financial outcomes? How did we come to accept this narrowing of purpose, and what are the consequences of such an acceptance?

In the broader scope of societal development, Mason's words resonate with even greater intensity. They challenge us to consider the long-term effects of this profit-centric approach on the fabric of society. If our educational leaders continue to prioritize revenue over education, we risk cultivating a generation educated in mechanics rather than thought, in process rather than discovery.

The implications are manifold and profound. Staff morale, as a critical component of any institution's health, is particularly vulnerable. When universities adopt corporate strategies, the shift can manifest in increased job insecurity, skewed resource allocation, and a pervasive sense of disconnection among staff and students alike. These changes erode the communal ethos that is essential for vibrant academic environments.

Thus, Mason's reflections on profit and purpose extend beyond corporate critique and into the heart of our educational systems. They compel us to envision a future where colleges and universities reclaim their noble pursuit—where education transcends the mere acquisition of knowledge and embraces its role in fostering holistic human growth. This vision, though challenging, is essential for ensuring that higher education continues to serve as a beacon of intellectual and moral development in a rapidly changing world.

RESPONSES

I believe strongly in the power of debate and the importance of bringing as many different perspectives and voices to a challenge as possible.

To that end, I have asked colleagues, friends, and contacts from a wide variety of professional backgrounds to read and react to the text you have just completed. My editing of their work has been minimal.

I hope you find as much value in their voices as I have, both in preparing this book, and in my professional life.

The Great Resetting

Carole Chabries, Ph.D.
Founder
The Clareo Group

You have them on your campus, too: Those recalcitrant faculty who disagree on principle with whatever is coming out of the provost's or president's mouth this week.

While the vast majority of faculty don't fit this stereotype, the reputation persists, leaving leaders muttering about damned shared governance and the dark side of tenure. Often the whole faculty body suffers, by reputation, from the persistent positions taken by the few grumpy old-timers.

In this context it can be tempting to pit crabby faculty against the more cheerful staff. I feel the temptation even more keenly after reading *The Admissions Counselor Malaise*, which is, among other things, an extended love letter to the "effervescent, engaging, energetic, and eager" admissions counselors who long "to connect with students" (15) and who bring genuine joy and caring to their work in enrollment.

Central to Teege's argument is the nature of a massive institution to exert its will in a creep so slow we barely notice its intensifying stranglehold, until the bright flash of an incendiary event illuminates the scarred battlefield of our lives. This experience was at the root of the despair felt by the post-WWII housewives at the center of Betty Friedan's The Feminine Mystique. It's also central to the restless misery experienced, post-Covid-19, by the admissions counselors Teege writes about in The Admissions Counselor Malaise.

I appreciate the structural and historical analysis that makes sense of our post-pandemic anguish as the consequence of inhumane institutions. (Hello capitalism! Shout out to you too, patriarchy! We see you.) I also appreciate the bold move of calling upon Friedan's (not uncontested) text as a lens for exploring ongoing experiences of widespread psychological abuse and gaslighting.

But perhaps what I appreciate most is the revelation of how much faculty (and therefore academic affairs) have in common with admissions counselors (and therefore enrollment). Having spent decades immersed in the institutional fragmentation that is a typical college's organizational design, I find myself moved to a deep sense of camaraderie I hadn't experienced before.

I wanted to be a teacher even before I was old enough to go to school. In my pretend classrooms I imagined my teacher-self in relation to students. That is to say I was a teacher because there were students: students who needed guidance, wisdom, and knowledge that I, in my expertise and devotion, could impart. I didn't fantasize about taking attendance, calculating grades, or chairing a continual churn of committees. I dreamed about teaching students, their eyes shining with excitement and new-found knowledge.

I'm not alone. After spending my career in and adjacent to academic affairs, I can confidently say that faculty generally love their students. They love classroom discussions about knotty topics. They love the creative energy sparked when students learn new ways to solve old problems. They love walking across campus and seeing a student's face light up with pleasure: "Hi Professor!"

And yet on many campuses that love of student growth – the very heart of teaching – is disregarded by the institution as its insatiable hunger for more revenue overtakes even the most purpose-driven aspects of our work.

Faculty want students to learn.
Institutions want students to pass their courses to protect their retention rates.

Faculty want students to have relationships with their professors.
Institutions want students to develop bonds to their alma mater so they'll be active donors as alums.

Faculty want students to have a solid intellectual foundation when they graduate.
Institutions want students quickly to find jobs or enter graduate school to protect their rankings.

For many years now - and notably since the pandemic - many campus staff and faculty (myself included) have pitched battles against individuals: evil overlords, toxic narcissists, and even lawbreaking bad actors. But Teege reminds us that those of us who love serving students are not simply suffering at the hands of a few bad leaders. We're suffering under the slow crush of institutional will.

Like a massive giant who somehow manages to creep up on us silently, the institution emerges as the villain of this story. Which means we can turn our fight to the institution, not (or not just) the small number of people in power.

By the time I had finished The Admissions Counselor Malaise I was imagining a new cultural watershed on campuses: The Great Resetting. Teege so skillfully guided me to this vision that I'm not even balking at its wholesale optimism. Teege makes me believe in the possibility of the Great Resetting as an industry-wide effort to reclaim mission and purpose and weave them back into our institutions' business designs.

Imagine if we made decisions focused on what truly serves students well.

Imagine right-sizing workload and re-assigning work to trained individuals with expertise.

Imagine taking an institution's most valuable recruitment asset: outgoing, energetic, engaging admissions counselors, and allowing them to spend more time with students and families.

Imagine the teaching parallel: taking an institution's most valuable educational asset – expert, trained, and passionate faculty members – and allowing them to spend most of their time with students and with their research.

Teege reminds us of the human experience at work: "Lacking meaning, we start to slowly unravel. If our work doesn't have a purpose that is in line with our values, we will disconnect from it, even if we go through the motions." (71)

Imagine leading a campus full of staff and faculty who feel truly engaged because their talents are used well. We all know the research: when morale and engagement are high, so is productivity and retention.

Imagine a world where admissions counselors aren't drowning in CRM data, and where faculty aren't squandering their lives in an endless cycle of pointless committee meetings.

Imagine leading an institution that, instead of slowly crushing its people, gave the gift of purpose to its faculty. To its students. And yes, even to its admissions counselors.

Imagine how that would influence the bottom line.

Imagine.

A Return To Simplicity

Kate Bittner
Independent Educational Consultant
Legato College Consulting

Upon reflecting on the insightful analysis presented in this book, the comparison between 1950s housewives and contemporary admissions counselors stands out, demonstrating how vendors and the higher education system have perpetuated a cycle of challenges and solutions that drive up costs in terms of both time and money. This raises the question of whether a return to a more straightforward admissions process is feasible.

The narrative reminded me of my own experiences in admissions, particularly during my time at Lawrence University, where my role in recruiting for the conservatory of music required deep engagement with students and families, fostering meaningful relationships that extended beyond the admissions process. These relationships formed the foundation of my "why" for this profession.

However, my promotion to Director of Conservatory Admissions shifted the focus from personal interactions to managing numbers and meeting faculty expectations through the ups and downs of admission cycles. This shift, coupled with personal factors such as relocation and the universal pressures of the pandemic, ultimately led to a disconnect from my initial motivations in admissions, prompting my departure from the field.

The support and guidance from leaders like Ken and Beth at Lawrence were invaluable, they championed the balance of personal well-being with professional responsibilities, emphasizing a team-oriented approach that significantly shaped the admissions process. This collaborative spirit is something I miss in my current role as an Independent Educational Consultant (IEC), where the nature of interactions differs significantly.

This reflection raises an important point about how admissions counselors in specialized roles, such as athletics, international, or music/fine arts, maintain a connection to their foundational "why", given the inherent focus on relationships within their positions. It is crucial to consider how the impersonal nature of modern recruitment strategies affects not only students and their families but also diminishes the role of school counselors who must navigate these data-driven environments.

The lack of personalized engagement in the admissions process contributes to increased stress and anxiety among students and parents, as evidenced by my interactions as an IEC. The positive response from families to personalized and warm interactions during college visits, particularly at Lawrence, highlights a broader industry trend where individualized attention is becoming the exception rather than the norm.

This book challenges us to critically evaluate these dynamics, examining how evolving roles within admissions affect both professionals and the families they serve.

Navigating the Tightrope

Elizabeth Kirby
Senior Director of Recruitment
Columbia College, Missouri

As I read through *The Admissions Counselor Malaise*, I grappled with the fact that enrollment management faces several tough realities. First, institutions rely on students not just for their educational mission but also financially—they literally keep the lights on. Admissions counselors are crucial in this equation; without them, we can't attract the necessary student body. However, when institutional changes clash with the motivations of these counselors, it dulls the enthusiasm of our frontline staff. We can all admit that while parts of it can be fun, being an admissions counselor is draining. Maintaining a cheerful, customer-service façade becomes exhausting when one's deeper motivation to contribute fades. We need strategies to align institutional goals with the motivational needs of our staff to sidestep issues like high turnover, disengagement, and a deteriorating office culture.

Support for staff needs to go beyond token gestures and we should focus efforts on providing meaningful professional development that fosters personal growth, encourages open and transparent conversations, and involves collaboration with peers or mentors outside our own institutions. By fostering a sense of community within this industry and making it accessible to our teams, we can bring a much-needed boost to morale.

One of the points in the book that resonates deeply is that institutions must realistically position themselves in the market. Many claims of uniqueness in marketing are not genuinely distinctive. This lack of genuine uniqueness can dilute a school's appeal in a crowded marketplace. We must find ways to differentiate our programs, faculty, and missions to attract students effectively. It's also vital to bring admissions counselors to the table to give them a voice and recognize their successes in these conversations.

Our system has drifted away from being student-centric as admissions counselors are expected to manage growing numbers of applicants using a multifaceted CRM and often multiple other systems with an ever-changing set of expectations. Forcing relationship-first interactions into a CRM system or campus culture that doesn't support them can be challenging. It's vital to ensure our CRM technology enhances, rather than hinders, the relationships counselors build. As the author notes, transitioning from a low-tech, high-touch approach to a high-tech, high-touch one can help. By utilizing our technology to better facilitate personalized interactions, counselors can spend more quality time with students, improving both their effectiveness and the applicant experience, ultimately making our institution more appealing to prospective students. However, these technological changes must be considered and implemented carefully as change fatigue just presents an added layer to the already complicated problem we are trying to solve.

More than ever before we have all witnessed that institutions are not safe from the realities of business as colleges across the country are closing. Reflecting on this showcases that we must have a heightened focus on revenue, as we have all seen what happens when we fail in that endeavor.

Reflecting on the countless challenges outlined in The Admissions Counselor Malaise, it is clear that the path forward for enrollment management is steeped in balancing institutional needs with the well-being of our staff. As I face these realities, I recognize the need for a reinvigorated approach that aligns our revenue focus with the genuine support and development of our admissions counselors. We must foster a workplace environment that not only recognizes but also energizes the intrinsic motivations of our team. By implementing strategies that enhance the support systems within our institutions we can better equip our counselors to manage their roles with enthusiasm and efficiency. Embracing these changes is crucial for sustaining our educational mission and ensuring the financial viability of our institutions, ultimately benefiting both our staff and the students we serve.

The Enrollment Equation

Nathan Ament
Vice President of Enrollment
Knox College

In the current educational landscape, small liberal arts colleges face a delicate balancing act. As the Vice President of Enrollment at such an institution, I am acutely aware of the pressures to increase net tuition revenue while ensuring we do not compromise the integrity of our educational mission or the well-being of our faculty and staff. Achieving this balance requires a strategic approach, underpinned by transparent communication and a steadfast commitment to our shared goals. This response aims to explore the challenges we face and the innovative strategies that can help us maintain this crucial equilibrium.

Small liberal arts colleges operate in a highly competitive environment where financial sustainability is increasingly challenging. The pressure to boost net tuition revenue is intense, driven by rising operational costs and the need to invest in quality educational offerings. However, focusing solely on financial outcomes can lead to decisions that may undermine the core educational values that define us. Balancing these financial imperatives with the need to provide an exceptional educational experience is complex, requiring nuanced strategies that do not compromise the welfare of our college community.

As we navigate these complex financial and operational challenges, we must prioritize role clarity and strategic alignment across all levels of our institution. It is essential that every member of our community understands not only their specific roles but also how these roles contribute to our broader institutional goals. By fostering a culture of transparency and mutual respect, we can ensure that faculty and staff feel valued and understood, which is vital for maintaining morale and productivity.

Our focus on role clarity has led to the development of comprehensive job descriptions and clear performance metrics that align with both individual capabilities and institutional priorities. This approach not only enhances accountability but also empowers our team by providing them with the tools and knowledge necessary to excel in their roles. Moreover, it fosters a sense of ownership and pride in their contributions, which is crucial for building a supportive and collaborative work environment. By clarifying roles and expectations, we help ensure that our faculty and staff are not overburdened or misaligned with the college's strategic objectives, which can lead to burnout and dissatisfaction.

Further, embracing a balanced approach means we must continually assess and adjust our strategies to meet the evolving needs of our students and the financial health of our institution. This requires a commitment to innovation and flexibility in our enrollment practices and financial aid strategies. For instance, by integrating advanced analytics, we can more effectively predict enrollment trends and student needs, which in turn helps us to optimize our tuition revenue without compromising on the quality of education or the well-being of our students.

However, we must also set realistic expectations regarding the amount a family is willing or able to pay. Historically, this seems to be in the $12,000-$15,000 range towards the comprehensive fee at most institutions. So, if this is the market price, we must address how we plan to educate (and house) our students for this amount. While this doesn't necessarily mean expense cutting, this does mean optimization of our operating and compensation expenses for what the future looks like for our particular institution.

Additionally, we must recognize the indispensable role of our faculty and staff in achieving these goals. Clear role definitions, consistent communication, and supportive leadership are critical. By clarifying the responsibilities and expectations of each role, we foster a more focused and motivated workforce. This clarity helps everyone—from admissions counselors to senior administrators— understand how their efforts contribute to the institution's overall mission and financial health.

Investing in professional development is another key strategy. When our staff feels valued and equipped to handle their duties, not only does job satisfaction increase, but so does their effectiveness in meeting the diverse needs of our students and the institution. This includes training that enhances their skills in areas such as student engagement, data analysis, and personalized communication, ensuring that every team member can excel within their defined role and contribute to the collective success of our college.

In conclusion, balancing the priorities of net tuition revenue, student needs, and staff welfare is a delicate task that requires thoughtful leadership and strategic planning. By establishing clear roles, investing in our staff, and continually aligning our strategies with the core mission of our institution, we create an environment where everyone can thrive. This not only enhances our ability to meet financial goals but also ensures that we provide the best possible experience for our students and a rewarding work environment for our staff. Ultimately, the success of our college depends on the harmony of these elements, driving us toward a future where education remains a transformative force for all involved.

Considering an Equity Lens

Paris Wicker, Ph.D.
Assistant Professor of Higher Education
State University of New York at Buffalo

The Admissions Counselor Malaise is a timely book that speaks to the broader implications about work, labor, happiness, and higher education. As the United States just recently fell from the top 20 happiest countries for the first time, this book focusing on the tensions with college admissions professionals, and speaks to a larger issue that many unhappy Americans face in their personal and professional lives. Those of us connected to college admissions know that many aspects of the system are indeed broken, as we continually ask more of students and families, and as Teege Mettille convincingly lays out, asks more and more of admissions counselors, often without the increase in support or pay.

While the book makes parallels between the current malaise with admissions counselors and the discomfort of the 1950's housework as examined in *The Feminine Mystique*, I would push the conversation even further within an equity lens to show how the demand to do more with less and even the ability to resist is unequally distributed with college admissions. Just as it was in the 1950's with discriminatory and exclusionary housing and mortgage practices that only gave certain woman and families the opportunity to the American dream, by looking at the most vulnerable admissions counselors and those on the margins (first-generation college students, those with disabilities, those who themselves have taken on significant educational debt) can we see the true complexity of struggles and challenges for this generation of admissions counselors so desperately seeking to make a positive difference and improve college access for all.

What I appreciate is that Teege Mettille treats this trend of discomfort, this "dis-ease" as a symptom of a broader concern and not the problem itself. I especially appreciate the return to relationality with one another as an opportunity to move forward. We are all related and what we do in one office, one institution, or one state has implications for us all. This book provides an opportunity for us to move forward as a profession, or resist change at our own peril. The successful recruitment, retention, and satisfaction of admissions counselors remains a vital component of the future of college admissions.

The Human Connection

Emily Smith
Vice President of Partner Success
CollegeVine

Amidst the avalanche of applications and endless clicks in the CRM, admissions has been reduced to a transaction, and counselors' work has been robbed of its soul: the human connection. Ironically, the key answer to the malaise is a thing without a soul at all- Artificial Intelligence. No, I'm not talking about replacing humans with bots. Chill.

Teege set it up just right: we're here because of institutions' rabid focus on revenue, which is at odds with admissions counselors' desire to be deeply relational.

Recently, I was talking to my first boss out of college, Topher Small. Topher began his career as an admissions counselor in the late 1960s, went on to be VPEM at numerous institutions, and retired as an enrollment consultant. As we chatted about the future of admissions, he inevitably started to reflect on students and parents he met 50+ years ago. He wasn't talking about these students in aggregate, he was recounting specifics: a junior and her father he met in the San Francisco Hilton and spent three hours with (three hours! A junior!), and a kid from Massachusetts who was accepted to MIT, but Topher convinced him that Ripon College was a better fit. This is the deep delight of the admissions counselor: Connecting, helping, evangelizing.

In his long career, Topher recruited decades of classes where the entire student volume was probably equal to some of our single-year applicant pools today. This was a human having human memories about a relatively small number of students that his human brain could remember in great detail. Given how funnels have ballooned, the present-day admissions counselor couldn't possibly hold these details in their head.

Topher took me to my first NACAC- 2004 in Milwaukee, which Teege mentions so frequently in the book. I've only missed one or two NACACs in the interim to have a couple of babies (hey, Betty Friedan! I found out what it feels like to be a homemaker/mother and a career woman: I'm tired and slightly bitter.) Since then, I've spent 20 years on the vendor side of enrollment consulting and admissions technology. I've worked with at least 500 colleges and universities on everything from Student Search to CRM. My biggest learning: colleges recruit better classes more efficiently, and admissions counselors are more satisfied when the enrollment operation focuses on more personalization and more relationship building at scale.

To become high touch / high tech, we must use AI to free up humans to do what humans do best and let the tech do the heavy lifting. AI is great at ingesting an enormous amount of information (far greater than what our brains can hold), and making excellent recommendations about how to treat a student. AI will allow an explosive evolution of nurturing prospective student interest and will be the turning point in the admissions counselor malaise.

This evolution will take us from where most enrollment operations are today: admissions counselors grimly turning the crank and serving prospective students bleak emails customized with their first name, offering paltry individual attention only after an app is submitted. It will scream through today's gold standard/ aspirational enrollment operation where students are bucketed into groups based on a mix of geographic, demographic and psychographic data, and get a more nuanced set of communications but still no transformational relationship with admissions.

Where we are rapidly heading with AI is a return to the relationship building of the past. Prospective students will have individual funnel journeys designed by AI and powered by smart algorithms that adapt and learn. Admissions officers will lift out of the CRM, be supported by AI's great recommendations for how to engage with students, and will be freed up to do what they do best and find most fulfilling: offer relational warmth and transformational connection.

Pressure Point: Counselors or Profit

Geoff Baird
Founder and CEO
Enroll ml

"If institutions cared about their staff or their students as much as they care about revenue, our jobs would look different."

This observation, echoing throughout *The Admissions Counselors Malaise*, underscores the pervasive shift in higher education from prioritizing student service to fulfilling revenue targets—a shift that has deeply affected both the roles within admissions departments and their broader future. While many of us in the field might nod in agreement, saying, "We've known that for a while," Teege's exploration sheds new light on the profound implications this shift has on the well-being of admissions counselors and the quality of the student experience.

Having spent years in the business sector before venturing into higher education administration, I approach the commercialization of higher education with a dual perspective. While Teege and I may engage in spirited debates about the merits and demerits of this commercialization, we converge on one critical point: the health and fulfillment of admissions teams are pivotal for the success of both educational institutions and their students. Yet, as it stands, the admissions profession is far from healthy.

Teege adeptly draws a parallel between today's admissions counselors and 1950s suburban housewives. Both groups grapple with external pressures demanding personal sacrifices for institutional goals, overshadowing their individual well-being. This comparison not only highlights the emotional and psychological toll on admissions professionals but also calls into question the sustainability of current practices.

Despite the challenges posed by an increasingly commercialized landscape, the essence of higher education still must revolve around broad and equal access to the nurturing and development of minds. However, with admissions teams under constant pressure to meet ever-escalating targets, the pivotal human element of guidance and support dwindles, potentially diminishing the holistic development of students and the successful (and critical) alignment of student and institutional objectives and outcomes.

So, what now? How do we reconcile the need for financial viability with the imperative to maintain an admissions team that is both motivated and content?

We must find a balanced approach, one that integrates revenue needs with genuine consideration for staff welfare. Institutions might, for example, develop and align new metrics for success that weigh financial outcomes, student outcomes and staff satisfaction. Additionally, adopting technologies like AI to streamline operations will reduce the strain on admissions counselors while preserving the human touch for students where it counts most.

In corporate life, balancing profit motives with employee needs was, and is a major challenge. And in my experience, listening to, understanding, and investing in employees' well-being has led to organizations that thrived both financially and culturally. There's no reason why higher education can't do the same. But it will require movement on both sides. The economic pressures on higher ed aren't going away. So now what?

Finding this balance in higher education is no small feat, especially in a landscape where the competition for a shrinking pool of students intensifies yearly. However, the future of higher education—and humanization of the institution by the admissions counselors—depends on our ability to redefine success. Not just in financial terms, but in creating environments where every member of the community can thrive.

Stopped In My Tracks

Angie Cooksy, Ed.D.
President-Elect | Host
Illinois ACAC | Elevating Admissions Voices Podcast

Warning: This book may connect you to feelings you weren't prepared to feel. If you are anything like me, you may feel mad, angry, curious. You may laugh and then want to cry. You may make a note about something you now want to research more about. Like I said...feelings.

This is not a book that just identifies a problem. Teege calls out the problem, names it, gives important context for how it developed, and inherently challenges the "way we've always done this."

I made it about halfway through page two before stopping in my tracks at his comment, "We are wrong to blame admissions counselors. The truth is we are collectively failing our admissions counselors." This book is filled with statements like this one that may give you pause. Statements that will make you think. Statements that will make you reflect on your office and the way your work is done. Bravo. We should be having these discussions, not in whispered hallway conversations, but boldly, out in the open to truly address the Admission Counselor Malaise.

Teege writes, "We can align the work that will help us achieve our institutional revenue objectives and fit the personal motivations and ethics of our admissions counselors." Living in the and. We can do multiple hard things at once. At the end of the day, my biggest takeaway of the Admission Counselor Malaise is that by naming it, we can impact it. In fact, it's the call of the book, "This book is written to be a clarion call for that reckoning." This is the transformational responsibility for our generation of Admissions leadership.

TEEGE METTILLE

THE ADMISSIONS COUNSELOR MALAISE

WITH APPRECIATION

This book has been quite the undertaking. At its conclusion, it feels appropriate to express sincere appreciation to some of the most positive influences in my professional development. While many of the ideas here are crossed over from my academic background and experiences as a Women's Studies major, my perspective on ethics in admissions, the importance of higher education, and the value of the work we do has been influenced by some truly great minds.

I will never be finished being grateful to **Ken Anselment**, currently Vice President of Enrollment Management at RHB. Long before that though, he was a young, excited, enigmatic admissions director who saw something and took a chance on me. There are many things I admire about Ken – his flawless public speaking skills, his mastery of the podcast medium, and his use of parenthetical interruptions (offering a knowing, tongue-in-cheek response to the text in the viewbook) are just a few. However, it his absolute commitment to taking an ethical approach to our work, above all else, that I've always tried to hold myself to.

There will also never be a time in my life that I don't feel fortunate to have been able to work closely with **Jim Miller** during my time at Northland College. Jim came on as an experienced, steady hand providing consultative support during a tumultuous time at Northland College. I had suddenly been given escalated responsibility and goals, and it may have been tempting to look for short, quick answers. Jim ensured that we never strayed away from the core underpinning of our work, regardless of the pressures surrounding us.

To my surprise, one of the most influential admissions leaders I've come to work with comes from the world of business, **Geoff Baird**. While Geoff and I take wildly different approaches to the same challenges facing admissions leaders – it is his innovative mindset that helps us find solutions, waiting in plain sight.

Finally, **Nathan Ament** is my co-host on The Admissions Directors Lunchcast, which is nice.

ABOUT THE AUTHOR

Teege Mettille is the Director of Enrollment Success at enroll ml, co-host of The Admissions Directors Lunchcast, and the Founder of Leading Colleges. In each of these roles, he has been doing his part to improve the challenging situation admissions counselors find ourselves in today.

Personally, he is proudly married to Derek, the love of his life – and is doing the best he can at being a father to Logan, who is just finishing his first year of high school.

TEEGE METTILLE

TEEGE METTILLE

THE ADMISSIONS COUNSELOR MALAISE

Made in the USA
Columbia, SC
21 January 2025

52204029R00121